BEYOND BOUNDS

CROSS-CULTURAL ESSAYS ON ANGLO,

University of
New Mexico
Press
Albuquerque

B E Y O N D
BOUNDS

AMERICAN INDIAN, & CHICANO LITERATURE

ROBERT FRANKLIN GISH

Library of Congress Cataloging-in-Publication Data

Gish, Robert.

Beyond bounds : cross-cultural essays on Anglo, American Indian,
and Chicano literature / Robert Franklin Gish. — 1st ed. p. cm.
ISBN 0–8263-1715–4 1. American literature—Southwest (New)—History
and criticism. 2. American literature—20th century—History and criticism.
3. American literature—Indian authors—History and criticism. 4. American
literature—Mexican American authors—History and criticism. 5. Mexican
Americans in literature. 6. Southwest, New—In literature. 7. Indians in literature. I. Title.

PS277.G57 1995   810.9'979—dc20   95-32548   CIP

designed by Linda Mae Tratechaud

To Albuquerque's South Valley, where I grew up "beyond bounds" in a cross-cultural world that made me who I am.

To Deb and Edith Wylder, with keen appreciation for their continuing encouragement.

To my friends all up and down and across the lines of Anglo, Indian, and Chicano ethnicity. To Eddie Sanchez, Eddie Gonzales, Carlos Torres, Sally Padilla, Joann Turner, Frankie Chavez, Arturo Chavez, Lucy and Edna and Irene Metzgar, Rosendo Garcia, George Davis, Patsy Burson, Terri Sangre, Betty Argo, Sharon Watland, JoAnn and Clifford McKinnon, and Kenyon Thomas—who danced the riffs and refrains of *la musica del Valle* with me, loud and soft, and I know still hear our mutual melodies.

And, ever and always, to Judy, Robin, Tim, and Annabeth; to Stuart, Matt, Joe, and Daniel, who travel the same expanding, at times confusing, boundaries of "family" in mutual love, hope, and understanding.

ACKNOWLEDGMENTS

I hope Mary Sue Coleman enjoys this book, which, in no small way, she makes possible with her encouragement, support, and abiding understanding of New Mexico and its special spirit of place. I appreciate the assistance of Orlando Romero, New Mexico author, who knows well the spirit and word-dance of the Gypsy and Lorca's *duende*.

My editors, Elizabeth Hadas and Floyce Alexander, are insightful, clear-eyed collaborators and have my boundless thanks and appreciation. Lynn Gamble showed me the way with cordiality and patience. Janice Rose and Zoé Brazil were most helpful and "cool in the clutch."

Warren Baker, Robert Koob, Glenn Irvin, and Paul Zingg have, for the past five years, made my tenure at Cal Poly conducive to experimentation and creativity and are exemplary colleagues.

Earlier versions of some of these essays have appeared previously in *The Bloomsbury Review, Cross Timbers Review, New Mexico Humanities Review, New Mexico Historical Review, North Dakota Quarterly, Re: Arts and Letters, The American Indian Quarterly, Minority Voices, Tamaqua,* and *Studies in American Indian Literature;* they appear here revised. Acknowledgment is also given to Confluence Press and the University of Nebraska Press, where variants of the essays on Welch and Lummis, respectively, first appeared.

CONTENTS

"The single greatest ally of those who would wreck the West is the idea that the West is homogeneous."
—CHARLES F. WILKINSON, *THE EAGLE BIRD: MAPPING A NEW WEST*

"The Southwestern experiences of the Indian, the Latin, and the Anglo-American peoples carry out of our earliest continental history into our own time the quality and dimension of the epic."
—PAUL HORGAN, *THE HEROIC TRIAD*

INTRODUCTION

These essays about Anglo, Indian, and Chicano literature reflect certain aspects of my own life and values, as a student of literature, a writer, and a person. In my own writing, in my occupation as a professor of English and director of an ethnic studies program, and in my personal relationships, I daily confront and cross countless lines, boundaries, and demarcations—and have done so since my youth. I know well that categories of place and distinctions of knowledge, of sanctioning and "belonging," are more protean than fixed, more imaginary and imposed than real. One's place on the academic, social, or cultural "bus" (back, front, passenger, or driver) changes with the times, as does the bus itself.

As a son of Okie-Indian parents who moved to New Mexico in 1929, and as a New Mexico native and citizen of Albuquerque's South Valley, I knew early on a peripheral perspective, of being beyond the bounds established and identified by geographical, cultural, political, racial, ethnic, and socioeconomic, even medical, centers and bestowers of power and preference. Such boundaries—the centers and edges—of these vast forces were and, of course, still are constantly shifting.

The center shifts, holds or does not hold, depending on the forces from the periphery—and the places in between. Admittedly, the "peripheral person," the "marginal man or woman or child," the "underdog," the "outcast" or "pariah," the "homeless," the "lawless" all have their own expanding, contracting, and blending boundaries, their own evolving and developing "centers" and natures in both kind and degree. Given my identity as a male and as a professor, many would look upon my titled and announced "place" in society as representative of the "establishment." Ah, but what is at one time or in a certain way inside the establishment may be, in other ways, decidedly outside it. Which is to say that whether one is inside the bounds or outside them is not always absolute. Change, as often observed, is the only certainty.

Because I grew up in the largest city in New Mexico, a sparsely populated, sublimely vast and "enchanting" state, at once an ancient and a modern place where indigenous peoples were conquered and colonized by Spanish, Mexican, and Anglo governments and cultures, mine is an inherently multicultural experience, perspective, and "life." In my youth and even today Albuquerque was not the cultural and political center of New Mexico and in that respect was peripheral to Santa Fe. And I more than once experienced the attendant snobbish presumption of that condition. And yet because Albuquerque was in the 1950s and is now in the 1990s the population, business, and commercial center in the state, the New Mexico city first blessed (or damned) by the coming of the Santa Fe railroad and other transportation and military technologies, in that respect I could share in appraising Santa Fe's eccentricities.

My home in Albuquerque's South Valley, however, was peripheral to the "City." I was a resident of the "County," and lived on a self-sustaining acreage with its own survival sources of both food and water in the form of a garden, an orchard, animals, irrigation, and drinking-water wells. The schools I attended were populated predominantly by Spanish-American and Mexican-American children. As an Anglo of mixed Irish, German, and Indian heritage, I personally knew in my South Valley locale "minority" status from the start. The Spanish language on the playgrounds was as much music to my ears as English in the classrooms.

My tastes in culture and music were shaped by rodeos and fiestas as well as by pueblo feast days and pilgrimages back to the Oklahoma hills, and hill-folk hoedowns, Cherokee ceremonial feasts, and story-fests.

My high-school and university education, at Albuquerque High School, New Mexico State University, and the University of New Mexico, was a blend of classical, European, American, and regional courses, a going and coming from schoolyard fights to student council, from studying Homer to hunting in the Rio Grande bosque, from Juárez border runs to ROTC parades.

When I wrote my dissertation on E. M. Forster and the Bloomsbury Group, I was the first to admit what my mentors intuited: I knew more of my father's South Valley gas station on Bridge Street and of my neighborhood drainage ditches than I did of London's Bloomsbury parlors or Lytton Strachey's quips.

It was from such geographical, cultural, and educational eclecticism, from what today would be called "diversity," that I developed my healthy disrespect for the confines of borders and boundaries. I cared not when, in the course of my career, certain specialists pegged me disdainfully as "interdisciplinary" or as a "generalist." American Studies seemed as bona fide as English Language & Literature. Since Jack Schaeffer's *Shane* was the first novel I ever finished reading, cover to cover; since I loved Frank Yerby's *The Golden Hawk* along with Emil Ludwig's *Napoleon*; and since I much revered the family editions of Emerson, the twenty volumes of *The Book of Knowledge,* our sundry obscure books of travel and exploration, along with the paperbacks and magazines and comic books my mother sold in her Bronco Cafe, I cared little for, nor acknowledged in any subservient way, any fixed literary canon—academic or otherwise. Respect and pleasure did not mean obsession or sycophancy. I grew up on Bridge Street and that was metaphor enough for my coming and going.

I surely felt from time to time the scorn of the establishment, elitist East for my southwestern hinterlands. But nativism holds limited rewards and I much respected *The Atlantic, The New Yorker, Harper's,* and *The New York Times,* and, thanks to the urgings of my teachers, I held no lasting reciprocal regional or subregional prejudices. "Cultural or personal recrimination never brings a second drink," David Hiatt, my freshman English instructor advised me, and his advice was echoed by others at the monthly reading and discussion groups he conducted at his home near the university.

In the Albuquerque Public Schools I team-taught American literature and American history. I taught remedial reading. And I taught Advanced Placement English. Each had its rewards. And as an instructor and eventually full professor of English and University Distinguished Scholar at the University of Northern Iowa, I developed courses in the History of Ideas, in British literature, and . . . in American Indian and Chicano literature. I risked the disdain of advocating, of "professing" what one concerned soul termed "Buffalo Chip Lit." And since critics were not imaginative writers, when I began writing fiction certain colleagues relegated me to the status of "entertainer," a category lower in certain hierarchies than "popularizer."

When, in California, I spearheaded the development of an ethnic studies program in a polytechnic university I scurried along the lines between the arts and the sciences, between disciplinary respectability (that is, objectivity) and allegations of "politicizing" a curriculum. Haven't you heard, I carped, along with Werner Sollors and Mary V. Dearborn, "American literature *is* ethnic literature." *Orale!* Yes, indeed, a person's reach should exceed the bounds, ere what's it all for?

Thus the essays collected here on a range of Anglo, Indian, and Chicano writers (none of them, finally, limited by designations as southwestern or midwestern or Rocky Mountain or western or ethnic writers) are for me very much "in bounds," and illustrate the ironies of this volume's title, *Beyond Bounds.*

So who is to say, ultimately, what is "in bounds" and what is "beyond bounds," what is at the center and on the fringes—especially in a time when boundaries are not only blending but disappearing. Call me a proponent of popular literature, or Western American literature, or ethnic literature, of imaginative writing and of criticism, of story and of history. It matters little. Inquiry, like quality, knows no bounds. Art is everywhere and forever. I take my cue from big Walt: "Do I contradict myself? / Very well then I contradict myself, / (I am large, I contain multitudes.)" After all, in a special encompassing sense, revered much by Bloomsbury, especially by Quentin Bell, history develops and art stands still, looming large, large . . . beyond bounds.

PART
ONE

ANGLO VISITORS

INTRODUCTION

How a place and its people are portrayed in literature depends on a complex relationship between the cultural values and perceptions of the writer and the "facts," the "reality" or "truth" of what is perceived. Through assumptions and methodologies of comparative culture studies, ethnic studies, and interdisciplinary studies, through the New History, the New Literary History, the New Ethnicity and the New American Studies, we are coming to "see" what was previously neither searched out nor seen in quite the same way: ethnicity, class, gender, and generational-regional cultures affect not just the style but the very substance of both story and history.

The literature of the American Southwest, not surprisingly, is filled with various and often conflicting ethnocentric assumptions about regional and ethnic meaning and significance. Anglo "visitors" to the Southwest do not define or experience "westness" in the same way as those who are born there or as those who view the Southwest as more north than west.

Although readers are perhaps the ultimate tourists, there are degrees of literary tourism just as there are degrees of belonging to a place or passing through it. All of which is to say that no one ethnicity, no one group—colonizer or colonized—offers the ultimate "truth" of tourism, seen most metaphorically as the "tourism" of mortality.

Such considerations about the complexity of ethnocentrism or homocentrism in literature are especially important when thinking about the writings, not to mention the lives, of Charles Fletcher Lummis, Erna and Harvey Fergusson, and Witter Bynner—all of whom exhibit varieties of Anglo arrogance in their interpretations of the Southwest, the place(s) they appropriated as their own. These four writers are, of course, mere representatives of the continuing influx of Anglo-American tourists-become-settlers in the Southwest—an influx that can be seen as part of the Anglo belief in Manifest Destiny.

The present-day culture conflicts in Santa Fe and Taos, in Albuquerque,

El Paso, Denver, Tucson, and Phoenix, may be more understandable when considered against the backdrop of Lummis's *Land of Poco Tiempo* writings about Mexicanos and Hispanos and Isletans; the Fergussons' rather paternalistic, albeit well-intended interpretations of the Pueblo Indians and the Penitentes; Witter Bynner's exclamations, sighs, and celebrations of the "Indian Earth."

Class is, of course, as much a factor as ethnicity in the interpretations of such writers. Rich and illustrious Anglo luminaries and writers are, more likely than not, most enjoyed by readers of a similar class and ethnicity. Admittedly, such stratification leads to some rather sinister barriers which all readers, all society must work to cross. But it is a good bet, nonetheless, that a majority of contemporary Chicano and American Indian readers will not warm to the assumptions and portrayals of their cultures by the Anglo elite of the early twentieth century or of the 1930s and 1940s, regardless of rhetorical stances. The biases shine through too readily.

I came to read Lummis, the Fergussons, and Witter Bynner through my reading of Paul Horgan, a kindred Anglo writer who had come from New York to New Mexico as a boy for his father's health and came to know the Fergussons and Bynner as friends and colleagues. Horgan, although younger and more removed in Roswell, was still very much a part of the Santa Fe and Albuquerque literati and the so-called Southwestern Renaissance of the first half of the century. Although Lummis is of no great regard in Horgan's career, Lummis did know and acknowledge the Fergussons.

What I recall feeling most vividly from my readings of Horgan is recognizing the place—particularly the city and environs of Albuquerque—about which he wrote. And I went on from Horgan's books and essays to read some of his circle of writers, his Anglo literary acquaintances. On one level it was heartening and beautiful literature. On another level, however, it was utterly alien to me in its sense of privilege and class and cultural control. And on that level I longed fervently to look beyond their Anglo visitations to hear older, less transient Indian voices, and see more angry and ardent indigenous Chicano vistas. It was a retroactive process, traveling back through history from my present, back to a kind of personal and societal future from my place as the son of Gringo-Indian-Okie, westering, ne'er-do-well parents, attempting an atavistic, blue-collar crossing of the bounds of cultural colonization and hegemony, going beyond my own dominant Anglo, Americanized acculturation. For a lad whose first comprehended novel was *Shane* and whose first writer hero was Jack Schaeffer, it was a long but increasingly self-confident search for regional and ethnic meaning in the most comprehensive sense—looking for enlightenment in the words and worlds of cross-cultural literacy.

CHARLES F. LUMMIS AND ISLETA PUEBLO

Charles F. Lummis's *Pueblo Indian Folk-Stories* is a book worthy of reintroduction. First published as *The Man Who Married the Moon and Other Pueblo Indian Folk-Stories* in 1894 and again sixteen years later under the title of *Pueblo Indian Folk-Stories*, Lummis's narrations of Isleta myths allow readers crucial insight into Pueblo cultures and into Lummis's own encounters with them as a major nineteenth-century Anglo adventurer and writer in the American West.[1] Now, a century later, Lummis's book commemorates both the Pueblo peoples whose myths and stories Lummis sought to perpetuate and Lummis's own love for the region of the West that he took credit for naming "the Southwest."[2]

In the 1990s, as centennial exhibitions of Lummis's first "tramp across the continent" and personal "discovery" of the Southwest are staged, and the quincentenary of Columbus's "discovery" of America and its indigenous inhabitants is both celebrated and condemned, it is especially appropriate to read *Pueblo Indian Folk-Stories*.[3]

Certainly Lummis was not Columbus. But in addition to characterizing himself as a "New Mexico David," he also thought fondly of the Spanish conquest of the New World, and particularly of Nueva Granada (the earlier designation of "the Southwest"). It is not surprising, then, to hear and take note of various Pueblo storytellers in *Pueblo Indian Folk-Stories* addressing Lummis as "Don Carlos," and for him to editorialize on the rightness of early Spanish dominion of the region.[4]

The Southwest and particularly New Mexico, true to its slogan as land of enchantment, always enchanted Lummis, invigorated him, healed him, and became part of his own life myth. In *Pueblo Indian Folk-Stories* these enchantments come vividly to life in a collection of thirty-two myths (folk stories) that center around the Pueblo of Isleta, which was then one of about twenty occupied pueblos along or near the Rio Grande. Other pueblos, particularly the Keres (Queres) pueblos of Laguna and Acoma (some fifty or so miles to the west), come into play in the book, as does Lummis's autobiography. Through editorial commentary and a kind of "Pueblo-deco" point of view, Lummis dramatizes his friendships and fascinations with the Isletans who tell him these myths, what he calls "folk stories," adapting and retelling them for a wider, presumably eastern Anglo audience.

In his original introduction to *Pueblo Indian Folk-Stories* Lummis equates "myth" with "fairy stories," with oral traditions that date back to the "childhood of the human race" (p. 1). In seeing Pueblo myth as fairy or folk stories Lummis suggests a certain juvenile quality of his own narrative adaptations. They are wisdom stories that explain ageless truths about the mysterious, interconnecting ways of humans, animals, and gods. Their "juvenile" quality is not so much substantive as it is descriptive of the dramatized audience of children seated at the feet of tribal elders.

Certainly Lummis's attitude toward the Isletans as "childlike" should not be misinterpreted as paternalistic, patronizing, or disrespectful. Although certain present-day readers might place a political spin on these stories and see them as a bit condescending in overall narrative tone and feeling, Lummis was decidedly much ahead of other Anglo Americans in his attitude toward Native Americans. Moreover, he clearly intended *Pueblo Indian Folk-Stories* as a tribute to Isleta and to Native American culture generally. In addition to the respect shown them in his writings, Lummis's legacy of the Southwest Museum near his eccentric rock-constructed residence, "El Alisal," in east Los Angeles offers further proof of his sustained respect for Native Americans, the sense of curiosity he felt about them and identification he felt with them.[5]

In an attempt to unify his collection of disparate stories, Lummis, from story to story, identifies his Isleta mythtellers as essentially seven elders who, seated around a winter fire at the pueblo or camped in the nearby Manzano Mountains, are variously introduced as Lorenso, Desiderio, Diego, Antonio, Felipe, Vitorino, Ysidro, and Anastacio. The respective narrators fuse into composites, however, evoking a kind of Pueblo chorus attempting to justify why things are so, and how they came to be. Adding to this chorus, Lummis is an ever-present intrusive narrator himself, intimately involved in listening and in telling and retelling.

If he favors any of his narrators, it is Desiderio—clearly his primary informant among not just the seven narrators but the twelve hundred or so inhabitants of Isleta when Lummis lived there from 1888 to 1892. For instance, in a frightening fantasy about baby-eating ogres, "The Hungry Grandfathers," Lummis's digressive frame narration soon overtakes the story of the ogres and turns upon Desiderio's discovery of one of the chimneys to the home of the ogres on Tomé Hill, located near a neighboring village north of Isleta. Of his friend and informant, Desiderio Peralta, who is also one of the first-heard narrators in the collection, Lummis says, "[He] could have furnished an army of old men with wrinkles!" (p. 219). Ideal readers will allow Lummis literary license in such attempts at humanizing presumed exotic and alien individuals, and attempts that unintentionally promulgate "according to an old Indian" stereotypes.

Aside from his narrative attempts to bring greater unity to the stories, a great many of them do reflect the ties of Isleta to Acoma and especially to Laguna Pueblo. This is no deterrent to the overall unified effect of the thirty-two stories, for many of them are thematically interconnected. The Laguna-Isleta kinship is of considerable historical significance to the ritual and literary traditions of the Isletans, and Lummis goes to some lengths to differentiate the Keres myths (Acoma and Laguna) from Tiwa myths (Isleta, Sandia, Picuris, Taos, and other Tiguex, Tanoan Pueblos). Moreover, he also attempts to separate post-Spanish myths, especially those that allude to horses or burros (animals introduced by the Spanish), from Isleta myths.

Pueblo Indian Folk-Stories, in its attempts at shaping and unifying Isleta and Laguna Pueblo myth in a single volume, helps readers understand why the Pueblo culture of the Rio Grande is so wonderfully complex. This complexity is enhanced by its ever-changing parade of interpreters and their respective attitudes and assumptions. In understanding Lummis's versions of more ancient stories, it is important to know that following religious splits at Laguna in 1881 many Laguna dissidents traveled to Isleta, where they were welcomed, and influenced Isleta rituals with Laguna kachina masks and other anthropomorphic myths and stories.[6]

Lummis, true to the history of both Isleta and Laguna, incorporates many myths that reflect these migrations and assimilations. In this context readers should note "The Moki Boy and the Eagle," "The North Wind and the South Wind," "The Sobbing Pine," "The Queres Diana," "A Pueblo Bluebeard," and "The Hero Twins." "The Drowning of Pecos" involves an even more convoluted retelling of Pecos Pueblo myth, heard in the pueblo of Jemez and retold to Lummis by an Isletan. It is because of such pan-pueblo stories in *Pueblo Indian Folk-Stories* that Lummis's insights into the larger Pueblo culture should be appreciated.

Most of the stories in the collection, Lummis says, were told to him in Spanish and many do reflect the three and a half centuries through which Isleta was influenced by Spanish dominion, especially by Catholicism and the Spanish language.[7] *Pueblo Indian Folk-Stories*, in its English retelling of Spanish accounts of Tiwa and Keres myth, affords intriguing linguistic lessons that not only enhance "local color" but go beyond it to help capture the many cultural laminations of the region. Lummis concedes much linguistic difficulty of Pueblo languages (for example, Zuni, Keresan, and Kiowa-Tanoan, which includes Tiwa). And it is important when reading the stories to note that such translations as exist in Lummis's retellings and in his narrator's Spanish accounts are as much attributable to his and the Isletans' fluency in Spanish and English as to their mutual fluency in Tiwa. Lummis, however, in his performance and presence as narrator, translator, linguist, artist, and anthropologist, is convincing in his insistence that he strives for essences, for the spirit of the stories rather than the letter.

In his translations and in his arrangements of the stories and the myth embodied in them, Lummis presents Isleta myths and rituals as examples of wisdom and initiation narratives common to Pueblo oral tradition. Here are stories, we are to accept (albeit in a slightly less innocent way than the children listening to them in the narrative formulations) that tell what happens when the strictures of the "Trues," the powerful Isletan deities, are violated. Ramon, Benito, Fat Juan (Juan Bischocho), and Tomás (as well as Lummis and the non-Indian reader along with him) are just a few of the innocents seated at the feet of the seven "viejos" (old ones) who serve up, usually through the offerings of cigarette smoke, special words to justify the verities of Isleta tradition. In a world of old men and boys the only contemporary Isleta woman is one Grandmother Reyes, whose female task, in "The Coyote and the Bear," is to unroll the mattress on the floor when the night's storytelling is over. As a *vecino*, or neighbor, Lummis stresses that he is privileged to sit by the winter fires smoldering in sympathy with the wordways that mark not only these long nights of the book's present but cyclical echoes of more ancient ones.

In the account of "The Brave Bobtails," a delightful "mythic" explanation of how the bear and the badger came to have short tails when they attempted to rescue a mighty Ute hunter, Lummis observes, "It has always seemed to me that the boy who always wants to know 'why?' has a better time of it among my Indian friends than anywhere else. For there is always sure to be a why, and an interesting one—which is much more satisfactory than only learning that 'it's bedtime now,' or that 'I'm busy'" (p. 177). Notwithstanding the reductive cross-cultural assumptions of such an endorsement, suffering to help a friend, although it means losing a tail, is decidedly an honorable act—a small price to pay.

The "brown story-tellers," as Lummis calls them, explain the "whys" of many things; why coyotes are always at war with crows and blackbirds, woodpeckers and bears; how rattlesnakes came to have rattles and poison while certain other snakes are harmless; why before and during the scalp dance there should be no thoughts of love; why arrowheads are called "thunder knives." Each of these Tiwa stories builds to "folk" explanations that find their truth in their beauty and invention as well as in their tradition.

Isleta as a place in these tales extends much beyond the Pueblo as center, into the Manzano and Sandia mountains to the east, and beyond them to the Llano Estacado, the staked plains known to the Pueblos much before these vast grasslands were marked by the Spanish. The dark, volcanic loomings to Tomé Hill, the plateau known as the Black Mesa that marks the southern boundary of the present Isleta reservation, the salt lakes in the southern Manzanos, the villages of Mesita and Los Padillas—all of these special and community-defining landmarks are given a special animism throughout. Personification of the moon and the sun, of stars and planets, of plants and crops (especially corn), of rocks, trees, and bushes, mesas and mountains, rivers and winds, landforms and elements, make for magical and compelling adventures; momentous odysseys of birth and death, of creation and destruction, trickery and gullibility, falseness and fakery deservedly undone.

"The Man Who Married the Moon," the original titular story of the collection, is an excellent instance of Lummis's predictions and his techniques as an adapter of Isleta myth. Several sequels of this story are interpolated throughout the other stories, amplifying this central account of one of Isleta's most charismatic and potent heroes. He is Nah-chu-rú-chu, a young weaver, wise beyond his years in medicine and healing. In his life, too, as in his art and in Lummis's, pattern and color and right action take the shape and the goodness of story. The identity of his bride and how he came to choose her take on much consequence for the entire population in those very early days of the Pueblo.

Nah-chu-rú-chu, along with other heroes, such as Antelope Boy, Corn Stalk Boy, and the Hero Twins, operate in a world where extreme remedies prevail. Nah-chu-rú-chu's time and world are long ago near Eagle-Feather Mountain in the Place of the Red Earth. In "The First of the Rattle Snakes" he suffers betrayal and transformation but ultimately punishes treachery and helps his people. The means by which he does so are dramatic; no halfway measures will work.

Besides cosmic, elemental, topographical, horticultural, and regional presences, there is much powerful fabulation in these stories. As for the bestiary represented here, animals take on significant roles both as characters and as exemplars much beyond any fatuous cartoons for children. Here we meet Eagle, Hawk, Beaver, Mole, Mouse, Coyote, Badger, Bear, Rabbit, Turkey Buzzard, Ant, Horned Toad, and Deer. All such creatures take on the larger designations of general human urgency, of life force and survival, of struggles between good and evil.

Taken individually and as a whole, *Pueblo Indian Folk-Stories* may be regarded as accountings of the continuing struggles for reconciliation between humans, with the gods, and with the natural world—the striving after some sense of wholeness and harmony. Lummis's "Tee-wahn" versions of Tiwa folk stories, like other Pueblo myths, offer words of warning and defeat, reaffirmation and triumph. These are stories not just by which the Isletans lived and continue to live, but a lesson and benediction, proof once again of the procreative power of story, itself a mythic inspiration. For this we owe Lummis our appreciation. Throughout the pages of *Pueblo Indian Folk-Stories* we can sense his own self-proclaimed but deserved pride in sharing his continuing legacy of "the Southwest" as he knew it and rendered it. His Southwest was a place, both permanent and changing, that he allows us at least partially to see through these nineteenth-century recountings of Isleta Pueblo. But who really was this man, and how did he come to write this book and to deserve to be remembered?

Whoever Lummis was before he went to his Southwest, and particularly New Mexico, he was never the same after "discovery." As it did D. H. Lawrence and so many others over the centuries, New Mexico remade Lummis and became—as place, as people, and as idea—his life myth. Even in a book of myths that center around Isleta Pueblo, Lummis's autobiography is obvious, for his prominence as narrator is everywhere dramatized: through editorializing, anecdote, and intrusive aside. *Pueblo Indian Folk-Stories* is directly tied to perhaps the most important period of his life, from 1888 to 1892, when Lummis actually took up residence at Isleta. It is a familiar transition in United States history and story: an easterner is transformed by the American West—and reciprocally transforms it in words.

Lummis was forever fascinated with words, with writing—a fascination waiting to be kindled by the vistas and spaces, the lives and landscapes of the Southwest. In Lynn, Massachusetts, as a boy, and later at Harvard University, indications were that writing would help direct his life's calling and the calling of the West. During summers in college he worked as a printer. After his marriage to Dorothea Roads and their move to Ohio, he worked as editor of the *Scioto Gazette* in Chillicothe. By arrangement with the *Los Angeles Times*, he contracted to submit weekly articles about a long sojourn by foot from Ohio to California. Once his trek had taken him to California, he worked as editor for the *Times* and later covered the Apache wars in Arizona.

In 1888, due to overwork and pressures of city life, he suffered the first of several strokes, which partially paralyzed his left arm, affected his gait and his speech and helped him decide to return to New Mexico—first to San Mateo, near Grants, where he stayed again with Amado Chaves, a latter-day Spanish aristocrat and New Mexico territorial attorney and politician whom Lummis had met earlier on his three-thousand-mile "tramp across the continent." Mutual accounts of their friendship confirm that their meeting helped solidify Lummis's claim to New Mexico citizenship, even when living in California. It was a friendship that, after his stroke, drew him back for a recuperative stay much longer than the initial week's visit in 1884. Most importantly, it was a friendship that positioned him for his move to Isleta and the recording of the myths in *Pueblo Indian Folk-Stories*.

It was, according to Chaves's account, Lummis's photographs of secret Penitente crucifixion rituals near San Mateo, and the printing of those pictures in *Scribner's Magazine*, that led to numerous threats on his life and culminated in an attempted ambush outside his Isleta house in February 1889. As printed in Lummis's *Land of Poco Tiempo* (1893), those photographs and their violations of sect taboo were the probable cause of the ambush and near-murder, and not Lummis's involvement in a range war as is also speculated. Whatever the causes of such danger and intrigue, Lummis's years at Isleta provided the stuff of his own life myth as well as the Pueblo folk stories.[8]

At Isleta, Lummis was drawn back into the mythic Native American and Spanish past. He had visited the pueblo on his original westering trip and had described his reactions to the ceremony of the "Fiesta De Los Muertos" (the Celebration of the Day of the Dead) in *A Tramp across the Continent*. In taking up residence there in a house rented from María García Chihuihui, the wife of Antonio Jojola, Lummis sought to explore further the culture and myths of this particular Tiwa branch of Pueblo culture.[9] He carried out his explorations at the pueblo by making photographs and by listening to and composing these "Indian fairy stories or folk stories," as he designated them. As the dedication to the book reveals, he created a lasting autobiographical bond to Isleta through meeting Eve Douglas there: "To the fairy tale that came true in the Home of the Tee-wahn, my wife and child."

During his stay at Isleta he divorced Dorothea Roads and married Eve Douglas, his neighbor and the sister-in-law of an Isleta trader.[10] Her delivery of their first child occasioned a report by Lummis on his relation with the Isletans.[11] The Isletans, Lummis asserted, thought of him as a wizard and, if not a witch, then at least bewitched. Although the natural cause of his paralysis and illness was a stroke, the Isletans, he said, believed that he should directly confront the witch who had cast a spell on him. His eventual recovery—due to "a powerful constitution and an outdoor life"—convinced his Pueblo neighbors that he had paid other witches to cure him.[12] His exposure to such attitudes helps explain the high incidence of stories dealing with bewitchment in *Pueblo Indian Folk-Stories.*[13]

Lummis's degree of acceptance into Pueblo inner circles is, as dramatized in the stories, quite extraordinary and perpetuates his own life myth as an archetypal Anglo-American initiate into Native American culture, a familiar myth in western literature. He portrays himself, too, through his footnotes and refinements of remote and subtle Pueblo meanings, as an anthropologist hero something like his friend and contemporary Adolph Bandelier. We are led to believe that Lummis is engaging in serious fieldwork in addition to producing literary entertainments.

Lummis's narrative personae—adventurer, writer, anthropologist, and friend—are not wholly imaginary ones. They were perpetuated in both his life and his writings. Lummis's life myth merging with Isleta myth is obvious from the very first story, "The Antelope Boy," when, as the narrative begins, he identifies himself as benefactor: "[Lorenso] pauses only to make a cigarette from the material in my pouch (they call me 'Por todos,' because I have tobacco for all."[14]

The history of Isleta Pueblo and its location in the Southwest of map and mind are a much larger story and process than Lummis's years of convergence with it. Isleta, the "island" pueblo, is rich in comparative Native American/Hispanic/Anglo cultures. Located twelve miles south of Albuquerque, Isleta has its own special historical and cultural fascinations, in part because of its proximity to one of the largest southwestern cities. Furthermore, Isleta's location on the north-south axis of Rio Grande migrations positions it at the historical crossroads of southwestern exploration and settlement—from much before the coming of the conquistadors, through the frontier and railroad periods, through the atomic age and into the space and computer eras of the twentieth century.

Its location on a lava mesa or promontory that was long ago an island in the Rio Grande gives Isleta its Spanish name, but it is also known as San Agostín, or St. Augustine, the name of its legendary Catholic church. The Pueblo's Tiwa name is Shiw'iba, or as Lummis designates it, Shee-eh-whib-bak—that is, "knife laid on the ground to play *whib*," a name coined from a foot race where runners carry a stick with their toes, and reminiscent of the fleet-footed contests that pervade the myths in *Pueblo Indian Folk-Stories*. Among the stories dealing with tricks and rigged races between animals, men, and gods, readers will find "The Race of the Tails" and "The Antelope Boy" of interest.

As described by Lummis in his introductory "Brown Story Tellers," Isleta at the time of his residence there was an idyllic place. It was "nearly surrounded by fertile vineyards, orchards of peaches, apricots, apples, cherries, plums, pears, and quince, and fields of corn, wheat, beans, and peppers, all owned by my dusky neighbors." He goes on to describe the Isletans as physically short and stout with "magnificent depth and breadth of chest, and a beautifully confident poise of the head" (p. 4). The actual census of 1890 reported the population of Isleta as 1,059. A century later, Isleta, one of the region's largest pueblos, is home for approximately three thousand people, many of whom work in the adjacent towns of Los Lunas, Belen, and Albuquerque. The Isleta reservation, geographically, extends from the Manzano Mountains west to the Rio Puerco, and encompasses 209,891 acres.[15]

Much of Isleta history, like that of the other Rio Grande Pueblos, involves the explorations and colonization of Spain in the Southwest. Consistent with his efforts to preserve California's Spanish missions, Lummis is, throughout *Pueblo Indian Folk-Stories*, in sympathy with Spanish dominion over the Pueblos. He does not question the assumptions of Spanish conquest. Certainly the anger and hostility of the larger Pueblo Revolt of 1680 is nowhere to be seen in *Pueblo Indian Folk-Stories*. In part this may be due to Lummis's intent to "transcribe" and reshape myths and stories for the instruction and edification of youths. And in fact, for reasons not fully understood by historians, Isleta did not participate in the original massacre of the Pueblo Revolt. The Spanish did attack Isleta, burn the pueblo, and take over five hundred captives. And during the revolt the move to Isleta of over a thousand settlers from the town of Bernalillo solidified Spanish control so that when Governor Antonio de Otermín and other refugees from Santa Fe reached Isleta they found the few Isletans who remained increasingly hostile. A small number of the Isletans were resettled farther south, near El Paso, at what came to be called Ysleta del Sur.[16]

Spanish records, especially the Benavides Memorial published in Madrid in 1630, show that the mission at Isleta was flourishing as early as 1629, having been established, in Catholic perception, in 1612 by Friar Juan de Salas. Readers interested in tracing aspects of Spanish influence in the stories Lummis narrates should take note, too, of the assumptions about witchcraft throughout. Although such themes are closely tied to traditional native religions, they also carry the colorations of Spanish colonization and religious conversion and heresy. Such stories include "The Man Who Wouldn't Keep Sunday." *Pueblo Indian Folk-Stories* thus suggests that, whether interpreted by Lummis or others, pure Pueblo myth is not easy to isolate, given the tremendous changes that Spanish Catholicism infused into Native American religion.

The Pueblo people afford an amazing example both of cultural preservation and of assimilation and adaptation to other controlling cultures, be they Spanish, Mexican, or American. And in *Pueblo Indian Folk-Stories*

Lummis serves up only versions of whatever truths these stories attempt to represent. In his original introduction to the book he acknowledges that

> Isletan secret inner religion is one of the most compli-
> cated systems on earth. Besides the highest deities, all
> the forces of nature, all animals, as well as many things
> that are inanimate, are invested by them with supernat-
> ural powers. They do not worship idols, but images
> and tokens of unseen powers. . . . They do nothing
> without some reason, generally a religious one, and
> whatever they observe they can explain in their own
> superstitious way. Every custom they have and every
> belief they own has a reason which to them is all-
> sufficient; and for each they have a story. There is no
> duty to which a Pueblo child is trained in which he has
> to be content with the bare command, "Do this"; for
> each he learns a fairy tale designed to explain how peo-
> ple first came to know that it was right to do thus.

Isleta culture and myth are merely part of larger Pueblo culture and myth and Lummis merely one interpreter of the traditional oral literature of the Pueblos. Current figures place the entire Pueblo population at about thirty-six thousand people residing in eight northern pueblos and ten southern ones.[17] Keresan, Tanoan, and Zuni are the major language groups. There are two dialects of the Tanoan language: Tiwa (which includes Isleta, Taos, Sandia, and Picuris) and Tewa (which includes San Juan, Santa Clara, San Ildefonso, Nambe, Tesuque and Pojoaque). Such variety of language and dialect and the attendant variations in oral tra-ditions in the respective societies illustrates how easy it is to oversimplify just what Lummis attempts in the stories reprinted here. As Spanish he-gemony diminished, English replaced Spanish as a language of accom-modation for the Pueblos. Revered communications still depend on tribal languages and "in the religious or classic languages, the vocabulary and terminology remain unchanged."[18] Lummis's oral retellings must essen-tially be seen as entertainments, themselves recast in the Spanish of an earlier century when Spanish influence was still compelling. Pueblo oral tradition and the myths and stories it imparts are, then, much more com-plex than Lummis's renderings, at first glance, might suggest. Among the more accessible books on Pueblo oral narrative performance, Dennis Ted-lock's *Finding the Center* helps demonstrate, in terms of Zuni narrative poetry, just how simultaneously simple and involved (linguistically and culturally and aesthetically) Pueblo oral tradition actually is.

If one contrasts Tedlock's and other anthropologists' accounts of their laborious and fastidious field studies of Pueblo languages and cultures with Lummis's descriptions of his storytelling sessions with the Isletans, it soon becomes clear that he was more the artist-raconteur than the social scientist. He is, he himself stresses, not so much interested in the letter of these stories as in the spirit. A literal translation, he insisted at the beginning of the 1894 edition, would be "unintelligible to English readers" but he also insisted that he took no liberties "with the real meaning." His control of the original myths and, now in the retelling, of his English-language audience is apparent. Contemporary readers will no doubt find ironies and distances (between Lummis and his personae and Isletan narrators; between author, and story, and reader) never dreamed of by Lummis. Lummis's methodology and result, we must acquiesce, offers us a text, say what you will about accuracy, we would not have otherwise. What Tedlock says about his own frustrations with the "truths" of translation may be applied to Lummis's stories and perhaps all stories as well: "nothing I could do would make [readers] experience these stories precisely as a Zuni does. But there is no single, 'correct' picture of a given story even from one Zuni to another."[19] It is, then, in keeping with much current literary theory and Pueblo oral tradition to find our own truths in these stories in the same way that Lummis did and that countless Isletans did before him and with him. In a sense, the telling is all and it is enough.

Anthropologists have generally paid more attention to Isleta and to *Pueblo Indian Folk-Stories* than have literary critics. Few literary critics or authors, with the exception of Hamlin Garland, have been drawn to Isleta. It is their loss. Along with commentary by such notable anthropologists as Alfonso Ortiz, Florence Hawley Ellis, Elsie Clews Parsons, Frank Cushing, and Adolph Bandelier, Lummis's literary, stylized encapsulations of Isleta myth and legend, although not always seen as scientifically authoritative, nevertheless should continue to attract readers interested in him and in Pueblo culture. His firsthand look into Isleta myth, into Isleta ritual as literature and literature as ritual, continues to fascinate "tourists" of a later century. In the ebb and flow of history, the point is not how scientifically accurate Lummis is in his recountings of Pueblo myth, but that at his particular point in time he chose to move to the pueblo and to become a mutual part of Isleta "legend." He carried through with the enterprise with much honesty, albeit the honesty of art.

Parsons records that when *Pueblo Indian Folk-Stories* came to the attention of certain Isleta leaders in 1927, some thirty-odd years after it was first published, the Pueblo council queried the possible informants and determined that the stories were "not very important" and were "mostly of Laguna [Pueblo], . . . got by Lummis from one Patrico, now dead."[20] In Parsons's account, however, it is clear that internal Pueblo politics and recriminations against an alleged tribal informant (Pablo Abeita) were overshadowing the actual and fictive "truths" of Lummis's stories. Any wider public revelation of tradition Pueblo belief is understandably discouraged and often, after the fact, defensively discounted.

All in all, what Lummis's first bit of bold tourism actually did was change his life and, in consequence, contribute to an attitude and set of assumptions much larger than Lummis both in its origin and in its final playing out—the romantic perception of the American Southwest as a sublime landscape with spectacular geographical and geological vistas, shapes, and spaces; an environment filled with wondrous flora and fauna; an exotic land peopled by dusky races of Indians and Mexicans with strange cultures and brave histories worthy of explanation, description, interpretation. Certainly he was not the first curious Anglo-European tourist to traverse the American Southwest who regarded its inhabitants in need of explaining by "us"—that is, explanation of natives by non-natives to non-natives.

Although, in varying degrees, most Anglo-European westering shares similar stranger-in-a-strange-land attitudes, earlier travelers, such as the conquistadors and the missionaries who preceded Lummis, were not similarly well intentioned. But whether drawn by curiosity or the urge to conquer, light-skinned "explorers" confronted dark-skinned "inhabitants"— alien forces in cultural and political contact, European exoticism transported to the new world.

Pueblo Indian Folk-Stories is part of that process. Even so, Lummis's "Tee-wahn" versions of Tiwa folk stories, like most myths, offer words and actions of fear and warning, of defeat and triumph, and of human affirmation. These are not just stories to which the Isletans listened, to which Lummis listened, but an inspiration to us all. They offer proof once again of the efficacy and healing power of stories as "word medicine."

It is important to see Lummis's self-celebrations of "The Southwest" in the crucial contexts of multiracial and multicultural understanding— that is, as an attempt to understand others. Lummis was one of the few Anglo-American writers to observe Isleta and comment on its positioning inside and outside time, its ambivalently welcomed and resisted transitions into the twentieth century. Hamlin Garland also visited Isleta in 1895—a year after *Pueblo Indian Folk-Stories'* first publication. For Garland, Isleta remained a dream, a fantasy, born of his reading, "not of [his] actual living."[21] Isleta, for Lummis, became its own kind of dream come true as seen both in his living there and the reading about it that *Pueblo Indian Folk-Stories* now again affords us.

ERNA FERGUSSON'S TRAVELS
TOWARD EXOTICISM

As with any subject of complexity and tradition, there are many starting points when considering the Southwest and exoticism. One obvious beginning is with the travel book or travelogue, for it is this genre which most explicitly attempts to account for the intrusions of light-skinned peoples in dark-skinned worlds. The twentieth-century travel writer Erna Fergusson and her first southwestern travel book, *Dancing Gods* (1931), offer a case in point in that both the book's theme and method place it squarely within the tradition of literary and historical exoticism.

Although she aspired to write fiction and worked for a time on short stories and on a novel about Malinche, the mistress of Cortez, it was as a travel writer in the first half of the twentieth century that Fergusson made her most significant contributions. Her best-selling work, ironically, was a book on southwestern cooking, *Mexican Cookbook* (1934), which stayed in print for more than fifty years and is today regarded as a classic.[1]

As a New Mexico writer of the 1930s Fergusson was a part of what literary historians of the Southwest generally term the Southwest Renaissance, that period in the twenties and thirties centered around the artist colonies of Taos and Santa Fe whose membership included Witter Bynner, Haniel Long, Willard "Spud" Johnson, Oliver La Farge, Paul Horgan, Mary Austin, Mabel Dodge Luhan, and, for a time, D. H. Lawrence. It was Lawrence, among moderns, who, in New Mexico and Mexico, most dramatically rekindled the exoticism of much earlier travel writers such as Gaspar Pérez de Villagrá; and it was Lawrence, along with Charles F. Lummis, who most dramatically pointed the way for writers like Erna Fergusson.

Lawrence's essays about the Southwest were especially significant in transporting and transvaluating some of the assumptions of Anglo-European and, particularly, British writers—and their exoticism of Empire—to the modern American Southwest. As an Englishman and as a modern tourist, Lawrence saw southwestern locales and, particularly, viewed Native Americans in a new, more empathic way—a way that set the stage for revisionist Anglo-American perspectives of the twenties and thirties such as those of William Carlos Williams, Witter Bynner, Erna Fergusson, and, later in the century, Frank Waters, John Nichols, Edward Abbey, Tony Hillerman, and others.

In his southwestern writings Lawrence is characteristically involved in a process of transvaluation, of taking something generally disparaged or just commonplace and holding it up to the iconoclastic set of values by which he lived. And this flip-flop is precisely why the Southwest and its native peoples were important to him. As a place and as an experience the Southwest would not allow itself to be taken for granted. It woke him up. It served as a source of insight and inspiration—just as it did for Fergusson. The contemporary Chicano novelist Rudolfo A. Anaya similarly describes his life as a writer in the Southwest as an "epiphany in landscape."[2]

Lawrence was always enthusiastic about epiphany in landscape, about spirit of place—as was Fergusson. Here is a portion of Lawrence's familiar but still provocative counsel to others if they were ready for the region's epiphanies, its inspirations, its revelations:

> The know-it-all state of mind is just the result of being outside the mucous-paper wrapping of civilization. Underneath is everything we don't know and are afraid of knowing.
>
> I realized this with shattering force when I went to New Mexico.
>
> New Mexico, one of the United States, part of the U.S.A. New Mexico, the picturesque reservation and playground of the eastern states, very romantic, old Spanish, Red Indian, desert mesas, pueblos, cowboys, penitentes, all of the film stuff. Very nice, the great Southwest, put on a sombrero and knot a red kerchief round your neck, to go out in the great free spaces!
>
> That was New Mexico wrapped in the absolutely hygienic and shiny mucous-paper of our trite civilization. That is the New Mexico known to most of the Americans who know it at all. But break through the shiny sterilized wrapping, and actually touch the country, and you will never be the same again.[3]

Lawrence came to the Southwest as a world traveler, an exile in exotic places: Ceylon, Sicily, Australia, California, New Mexico. His reaction to the exoticism and epiphany of the Southwest? He states it this way: "The moment I saw the brilliant, proud morning shine high up over the desert of Santa Fe, something stood still in my soul, and I started to attend. . . . In the magnificent fierce morning of New Mexico one sprang awake, a new part of the soul woke up suddenly, and the old world gave way to a new" (p. 142).

Stanley Walker, of another, less effusive and less exotic mind and mood, took it upon himself in a *New Yorker* piece to complain about Lawrence and his brand of exoticism, his lyricism, a style he equated with "babbling," and which he said was shared by Erna Fergusson and others of the same tradition—all victims of what might be called the "Southwestness" of the country and thus the result of a style that Walker satirically called "New Mexico baroque":

> One either thinks "New Mexico baroque" is great or one doesn't. An odd thing happens to writers who live in the high country, especially in the mystical stretches along the Rio Grande above El Paso. It happened to poor old D. H. Lawrence, to Mabel Dodge Luhan, and to many others—to a lesser degree to such a sound citizen as Miss Erna Fergusson. They see the mountains, the sand, the stars, the cactus, the wrinkled Indians, and they begin to babble about "time" and "space." At best, and in moderate doses, this can be fetching; at its worst it can be baffling—like something by Dylan Thomas out of Sitting Bull.[4]

Never really the Baroque babbler Walker claims, Lawrence simply said, "for greatness of beauty I have never experienced anything like New Mexico" (p. 142). A large part of that experience were the Native Americans Lawrence encountered in the Southwest. They influenced him greatly—as they did Fergusson. And that influence was essentially exotic. Lawrence's English colleague, W. Somerset Maugham, defined exoticism this way—albeit in relation to the tradition of the English short story: "[The exotic story] is the story, the scene of which is set in some country little known to the majority of readers, and which deals with the reactions upon the white man in an alien land and the effect which contact with peoples of another race has upon him."[5]

For Lawrence the American Indian was religious in the oldest and deepest sense of the word, "a remnant of the most deeply religious race still living" (p. 144). It is such a sense of religion, of "God as red," which permeated the New World spirit of place that Lawrence found in New

Mexico. Thus his description of various Pueblo dances at Taos and at San Felipe function as the dramatic climax of his New Mexico essay. For five lyrical paragraphs, nearly two full pages of text, Lawrence tells of his memories of the dances. "Never shall I forget," he says. "Never shall I forget"—five times he repeats the phrase in balanced sequence, echoing the rhythms of the drums and chants and the dance steps as he tells of what strange sights he saw and what they meant to him as a prophet of "blood consciousness." William Carlos Williams, in *In the American Grain* (1925), and especially in his account of the discovery of Kentucky, picked up and perpetuated something of the same empathic identification with Native Americans, by focusing on Daniel Boone's "primal lust" and regenerative passion for the New World—a lust and passion that Williams saw as Indianlike; an élan unknown (in Williams's assessment) to Puritan and many Spanish perceptions of North America.

In her writings about the American Indian tours she took and often guided, and that resulted in her books about the Southwest, Fergusson was trying to explain a similar sense of wonderment, fascination, and "exoticism" that writers like Lawrence and Williams felt. Fergusson does not quite reach the same level of lyricism that Lawrence and Williams do. She is not a tourist like Lawrence—rather she is a guide, someone born to a familiar but nevertheless exotic place: the Southwest.

As an Anglo and as a woman, she tells of brave and beautiful things, just as other travelers had done before her, in the far-off places of the world wherever colonialism or other forms of "tourism" occurred. Lawrence and Williams were trying to express essentials, not surfaces. And so was Fergusson. Her brother, southwestern novelist and historian Harvey Fergusson, attempted to account for his epiphany of landscape, his sense of the exotic, in *Rio Grande* (1931), his collection of a dozen historical essays published first serially and later as a book. As he saw it, the ostensibly strange and remote, the quaint, the picturesque so familiar in tourism publications had little to do with the real Southwest, its essence. The rich and living background, which even casual observers could sense in the Southwest as "exotic" in the negative, ethnocentric, Anglo-European sense of the word, was, in transvalued truth, at the heart of the American experience—of America as a new world and of the Southwest as its Native American essence.[6]

Dancing Gods represents Erna Fergusson's best account of the Native American presence in the Southwest—her travels into exoticism. Her other travel books after *Dancing Gods* seem only to replicate it, although she wrote for the larger ends of defining an entire region in *Our Southwest*; and in *New Mexico: A Pageant of Three Peoples*, for the more focused purpose of describing her home—New Mexico. She wrote repeatedly about her travels through the Southwest and South America, but it is *Dancing Gods* that best captures the kind of travel book she was suited to write, the kind of book that, in a special way, allowed her the opportunity for her own kind of exotic "dancing."

No less a critic than the late Edmund Wilson, identifying himself as an easterner and as a journalist rather than an anthropologist or a Santa Fe aesthete, attributes his traveling to Zuni Pueblo in 1947, to see the Shalako ceremony, to the influence of *Dancing Gods*.[7] Wilson's own account of his trip to this famous pueblo—in its own right an exemplary piece of travel writing—offers good evidence as to just what kind of audience Fergusson had in mind when explaining the exotic ritual and ceremony of Southwest Native American dances: someone appreciative of powers of description, a person of intelligence, of respectful sensitivity and curiosity, and one desirous of making the journey into the dark-skinned, primal world of southwestern Indians. Just as Fergusson relies on numerous scholarly resources, so too does Wilson rely on Fergusson's book as his primary resource and guide. That he relied on Fergusson as more than mere motive in his seeking the exotic wonders of Shalako is obvious enough because he quotes extensively from *Dancing Gods* in an attempt to explain and understand the ceremony.

One can only assume that Fergusson appreciated Wilson's commentary and the mutually shared sense of what Wilson calls the "spectacular," the difficulties that he describes in getting to Zuni and in finally seeing such an exotic phenomenon as the Shalako ceremony before it possibly disappeared. In his words, "The journalist like myself, who has reported many hateful and destructive events, wants to get a good look at Shalako birds, bringers of happy abundance, before they shall have ceased to come, and before the bad liquor of the white man and the worship, perhaps of some white Führer shall, even for the Zunis, have taken their place" (p. 68).

That such destructive forces are at work, not just in the Europe of world war but nearby, is apparent in Wilson's description of his jumping-off place, Gallup: "The town of Gallup in northwestern New Mexico is one of the most forbidding stops on the Santa Fe railroad. It is a trading post and coal-mining town of the dismal and grimy kind, and the place to which the Indians resort to buy the liquor they are not supposed to have. They get drunk, have their wallets stolen, and come to in the morning in jail" (pp. 8–9). Wilson shares Fergusson's sense that in traveling to Pueblo country, in contrast to the squalor of Gallup where, under white governance, things have generally gone amok, they are experiencing something wondrous and worth recording from their Anglo perspectives (easterner and westerner, respectively)—for other Anglo readers to be sure, and maybe, given Wilson's picture of Gallup's aberrations, for certain lost Native American souls numbed to the "happy abundance of the Shalako birds."

Although Fergusson romanticizes the Shalako ceremony considerably more than Wilson, both of their Zuni travel accounts reflect a certain tough-mindedness and satire, a kinship that must have contributed to the influence of Fergusson's book on Wilson. As Wilson's essay on Zuni suggests, Fergusson was, in her written tour of Zuni, on the road to something significant for culture generally, for a larger white civilization in need of something as exotically redemptive as the Shalako birds. This urgency of need is stated in her purpose for writing *Dancing Gods* and the research and travel behind it:

> This book attempts to give a description of the principal southwestern Indian dances, based upon observation, and an account of their significance, based upon all available sources of information. It is not an exhaustive study, for several reasons, the most important of which is that the material available is not exhaustive. A few scientists have made detailed studies of a few of the southwestern Indian dances. I have consulted those authorities, I have seen most of the dances which are open to the outsider, I have talked with many people, both whites and Indians, and I have concluded that nobody knows all about Indian dances, not even Indians. (p. xv)

Fergusson explicitly identifies herself as an outsider. She appreciates the paradox that although born in the Southwest, she is an outsider through facts of race and culture. But she is a reflective and resourceful, an empathic "outsider." She knows that she is something of a trailblazer, a guide, a personal observer in pursuit of something combining social science with art, scholarly consensus of the time with individual subjectivity, history with story, science with art. She does not presume that she knows more than the Indians about their own dances and ceremonies, but she suggests that she knows something special *about* the dances—at least as much as she is able to discover in her own non-Indian way of knowing. Her implicit premise is that she knows and recognizes the dances as "exotic." Dancing for the gods and with them is one thing. Describing and explaining in writing what she sees is something else again. As a stranger in a strange culture she seeks to keep these realizations in the forefront.

Fergusson stipulates in her initial definition of terms that "an Indian dance . . . is a ceremonial, a symbolic representation, a prayer" (pp. xv-xvi). Drawing attention to religious dramas throughout history—from Hebraic to Greek to early Christian to medieval and modern ceremonies—she insists that the Zuni dance is both dramatic and religious. Reflecting the liberal attitudes of her era in relation to benefiting Native Americans, particularly the lobbying efforts of Santa Fe and Taos artists and writers and of theorists and policymakers like John Collier and Edgar Hewett, Fergusson suggests that part of her role as traveler/writer is to help preserve the Native American dances as an art form in the midst of the separation she sees taking place between the religious aspect of the ceremonies and the artistic: "In time, as Indians are weaned from their ancient faiths, it is likely that all their ceremonies will lose meaning . . . , and it is important that interested white people should help them to preserve their dances as an art form when they no longer serve as a religious form" (p. xxiii).

Apparently, Native American ceremonials had little if any personal religious significance for Fergusson—unlike Lawrence who ostensibly saw a much stronger vitalistic kinship, and one not assuming eventual assimilation. The significance of Native American ceremonials to her personally was, it is assumed, primarily aesthetic. And the assumptions behind her dichotomy of functions is decidedly ethnocentric. Whether or not American Indians would want to maintain an organically religious ceremony only as "art" was problematic in Fergusson's era and even more so now. In the worst light, to assert that Indian ceremonials be continued for their artistic aspects also suggests performance for Anglo entertainment. Nevertheless, it is a premise on which much of *Dancing Gods* is based and to some degree explains the motivation behind Fergusson's descriptions and interpretations of what she sees as "exotic."

She organizes *Dancing Gods* around the dances—seasonal in their purpose and occasions—of the Pueblos, the Hopis, the Navajos, and the Apaches. After a few background pages dealing with the history and the religion of these cultures, she describes thirty or so major dances that non-Indian tourists are allowed to see. Her intent is to re-create as closely as possible the sensations of such an experience to the audiences of the dances and the book itself. She is aided in this attempt by the various photographs of paintings by sixteen prominent New Mexico artists. Of the dozen or so various seasonal Pueblo dances she painstakingly details, the Zuni dances—according to Edmund Wilson—are the most meaningful and, to Fergusson, the finest and most exotic.

Just why she regards the Zuni dances as superb is in part due to the Zuni allowing visitors to watch the masked dances she so admires: "The distinctive feature of Zuni dances is the masks, which are more elaborate, more varied, and in every way more highly developed than any made by other American Indians" (p. 71). And she regards the Zunis as the world's best artists in the making of masks. (The Zunis, in the spring of 1990, finally declared the Shalako dances closed to the public—to tourists who had ignored the guidelines of common courtesy established by the Pueblo elders.)

Much of what makes her descriptions so believable is her staging of the scene in quite personal, diarylike terms. The reader soon is convinced that the author is no ordinary, gaping tourist; rather she is a determined, persistent artist in her own right, waiting to stay the extra day or awaken before dawn to experience all the preparations from the best possible vantage point. For example, in preparing herself she also prepares her reader, a silent but enthralled traveling companion, for the fifth day of the Sword Swallowers' dance:

> Wishing to see the very beginning of the big day,
> we got up before dawn and went to the sacred plaza.
> Crossing the village was an eerie walk. It was cold.
> Lights in only a few houses. No sound at all. Occasion-
> ally a blanketed figure slipped from a door and melted
> into the shadows, not seeing us. We made ourselves as
> comfortable as we could with many blankets in a cor-
> ner of the deserted plaza and waited. (p. 79)

The short sentences with their fragmented effect give the obvious impression of the actual walk, the silence, and the cold. The anticipation is heightened by a certain kind of reverence combined with curiosity. But descriptions of the Sword Swallowers' dance, effective as they are, fall short of the report and commentary of the even more exotic Shalako ceremony.

Fergusson notes that the Shalako ceremony does not have a definite date but always takes place between late November and late December. And she gives a comprehensive explanation of the preliminaries, the ceremony itself, and its aftermath—making clear that all of the stages are related and that as the greatest of all Zuni festivals it marks the culmination of the ceremonial year and functions as a prayer for continued blessings of fertility and harvest. Commemorative of the winter solstice, preparations for the extravaganza continue throughout each year. Forty-nine days before the ceremony, preparations begin with persons designated to represent Sayatasha, a rain god, and the leader of the Mudheads (kachinas in the role of clowns), each responsible for counting down the days until the Shalako come. Fergusson is deliberate in not immediately identifying and defining the Shalako dancers, their giant birdlike costumes, their clacking beaks, and the meaning of the term *Shalako*. Rather she builds—small detail by small detail, ritualized step by ritualized step—a composite picture of these special "dancing gods," the atmosphere in which they come, and the overall meaning of their appearance insofar as it can be expressed in words. M. Wright Gill's magnificent painting of the Shalako figure appears strategically in the center of the narrative, serving subliminally to coincide with the arrival of the six Shalako and Fergusson's attempt to describe them and explain their actions.

In preparation for the gods' arrival, special Shalako hosts and houses are chosen with special rooms, at a minimum of sixty feet long, and are made ready to greet the Shalako and entertain them. Focusing her descriptions on the last day and the great event itself, Fergusson heightens the sense of exotic wonderment by the use of such words and phrases of inexpressibility as "women do unmentionable things to their insides" (referring to the insides of sacrificial sheep), and "odors of fresh bread and freshly killed meat and cedar fires and close rooms are indescribable" (94). Precisely because their descriptions are "unmentionable and "indescribable" the point is made and the effect achieved: the ceremony is inexpressive of words—ultimately beyond the potential of exposition. Adding to the suspense and the spectacle of it all, Fergusson adeptly describes the audience gathered on the "great day":

> During the last day everything is finished. . . . Everything has been swept, food is ready, and people begin to appear in their best clothes. All day visitors drift in—long-legged Navajos on ponies, the women sitting astride in their voluminous skirts, the men wearing beaver-skin caps; Indians from the Rio Grande pueblos with turquoise to trade; Hopis with ceremonial garments; and a complete assortment of white-man types, from families of Mormons from the near-by towns to the Greenwich Village aesthete and Eastern tourists in stiff city clothes. (p. 96)

As author and "guide" Fergusson herself is both among and above such visitors. In this instance she knows more, not all, but more than the other visitors, at least the eastern tourists. Both the implied reader and the visitors are less informed. But in the universal scheme of things, the reader as actual rather than a vicarious visitor will become more nearly initiated as a result of book travel, of reading *Dancing Gods*. Fifty years after the recording of such a particular yet idealized ceremony, the Shalako as one Anglo-American traveler recorded it still lives, print becoming its own reality.

The actual entry of the council of gods who prepare the houses for the visit of the Shalako are all that Fergusson's suspense (the visitors' and the reader's anticipation merging) has made us hope for. What Americanist Wayne Franklin might call the traveler's confrontation with inexpressibility, or F. Scott Fitzgerald our "capacity for wonder" is addressed directly by Fergusson's use of anecdote in relation to the meaning of the word *gods*. Fergusson cites anthropologist Matilda Stevenson's adoption of the term *gods* for the Shalako in 1879; and then the author recounts the insistence of a Zuni woman that they are not "gods" at all but something entirely, lexically different:

> "They are not gods," said she; "that word is wrong.
> The Zunis have no gods; they are Ko-Ko."
> "Just so," said I, expectant pencil poised, "and
> what is the English word for Ko-Ko?"
> "There is no English word for Ko-Ko. I do not
> know. It is something different. I cannot tell you how it
> is to the Zuni, but they are not gods." (p. 98)

Through such a dialog and in her continued explanations, Fergusson succeeds in throwing into ironic relief her own ethos as an "authority," and the title of her book, *Dancing Gods*. What she is describing are not "gods" at all. To speak of dancing "gods" is to speak of the wrong thing; something too exotic, too inscrutable, be it "Ko-Ko" or "gods" or something else, some other word. Here is how Fergusson faces up to such bafflement:

> So there it is, as inexplicable as everything Indian must
> always be to the white man. They are not gods; they
> are Ko-Ko, and for Ko-Ko there is no English word,
> and presumably no English idea. It seems likely, from
> many similar conversations and a sincere effort to get
> the Indian point of view, that the Indian has no anthro-
> pomorphic gods. Yet such creatures as these of the
> Zuñis impersonate something divine: possibly merely
> an aspect of the great hidden spirit, which in one mani-
> festation is so brilliant that the sun is a shield to hide it.
> (p. 98)

Only after such a mystery of word and ritual is confronted by Fergusson the traveler and recounted for the reader is the spectacular entrance of the Shalako described. In such pacing and arrangement is a masterful instance of exposition and narration, one which brings the Shalako episode to a beautiful climax. Nothing in *Dancing Gods*, or for that matter in all of Fergusson's Southwest travel writing, is as startling and dramatic as her pages on the Shalako ceremony—most notably the actual appearance of the Shalako on one special evening:

> In a breathless moment of the swift winter dusk the Shalako appear. They come into sight round the shoulder of a hill, looming, as it were, on the far side of that deep impassable gulf which forever separates the mind of the Indian from the mind of the white. The six magnificent figures tower above their attendants; the eagle-feathers of their fantastic head-dresses raying like the sun, their flat turquoise faces and upper bodies swaying, their feet looking incredibly tiny under the hoop skirts of the double Hopi kirtles. They are about nine feet high, the tallest masks recorded. . . . The turquoise face is matched by a breast piece, and the white and blue are accentuated by a ruff of shining raven's feathers and by long, black hair. The mask is carried on a long pole hidden under the draperies and steadied by a man who also manipulates strings which roll the great bulging eyes and clack the wooden beak as the figure moves.
> (pp. 99–100)

After what Fergusson describes as much precarious swooping and dipping of these giants, and after they cross the causeway constructed across the river to their sacred resting place, she follows them into the houses that have been fashioned for them, to await their reemergence at midnight when sustained dancing begins. Fergusson's description of the close quarters in the Kotemshi house is presumably intended to provide a kind of "comic" relief to the majesty of the Shalako's entrance. Although the ways of the Shalako and the ways of men are successfully contrasted, the means are too harsh. She portrays the Navajo guests as "unwashed," greedily hungry. Trying, perhaps, to dramatize the incongruity involved in this meeting of two worlds—Native American and Anglo—Fergusson describes the effect of the Navajos on the non-Indians in these terms:

> Nowadays only the most intrepid white, or one well protected by smelling salts, can bear it long. Generally white visitors drift in and out; in when the cold with-

out seems unbearable, out when the thickness of the indoor air forces them to face the cold again . . . but aside from this movement near the doors, the audience sits all night, quiet and attentive. By midnight many of the restless whites have left and deterioration has begun to attack those who remain. Ladies' city hats are riding at queer angles, figures which started alert and trim have settled awkwardly among the aborigines, men in proper clothes and spats are huddled into the welcome warmth of borrowed blankets. (p. 103)

Satirical perhaps. But not really funny. Here, as in other portions of her travel writings, the limitations of Fergusson's ethnocentrism are baldly apparent. The "deterioration" in dress and demeanor that "attacks" the remaining see-it-to-the-end whites suggests the contagiousness of primitivism as somehow inevitable after prolonged experience "among the aborigines." For today's readers, such passages—although effective in personalizing the event—reveal the strain of seemingly subconscious, deep-seated condescension toward Native Americans, especially the Navajo, to which an avowed "Indian" partisan like Fergusson was somehow ironically oblivious.

Such moments are few in Fergusson's remaining summation of the Shalako ceremony as it extends over five more days of festivity and the offering of mounds of food and clothing and trinkets given to the Koyemshi for their part in the ceremony. The visitors leave and are long since gone into history. But the motive and method of the Shalako ceremony continue—in the now secret yearly rituals of the Zuni, and in Erna Fergusson's amazing travels toward exoticism experienced and recorded in *Dancing Gods*.

HARVEY FERGUSSON'S LEGACY

Stanley Walker's *New Yorker* indictment of certain "New Mexico" writers thirty years ago (see p. 18) still rankles us today. Walker did not like their literary style, which he called "New Mexico baroque," and said so. The occasion for this not entirely playful criticism was Walker's review of Paul Horgan's *Great River* (1954). Walker's title—whether his own invention or his editor's—gives one the drift, so to speak, of what he thought of the Rio Grande and of Horgan's style: "Long River, Long Book." Walker lamented what was *in* and what was *out* of *Great River*; *what* was said and *how* it was said. Remaining unconvinced about Horgan's picture of the Rio Grande as the stage for the recurrent and sequential frontiers of American Indian, Spanish, Mexican-American, and Anglo-American cultures all attempting to share in the making of what he called "a neighborhood of the world," Walker pictured Horgan like Erna Ferguson and D. H. Lawrence as merely another delirious New Mexico writer suffering from, according to Walker's metaphor, the ailment of "New Mexico baroque":

> It is just the old New Mexico writer's fever coming up
> again while the mirages dance on the high mesa, the
> tomtoms boom in the moonlight, and the gods cavort
> on the red peaks. Pretty, but is it history?[1]

One might dismiss Walker's glib attack as entertainment, countering with the question, "Cute, but is it criticism?" One could dismiss him out of hand if it were not for a nagging awareness that there is something to what he says about the effect that New Mexico—as inspiration and source material, as landscape, as geography, as what Lawrence so often stressed as "spirit of place"—has on writers (novelists, poets, and even historians). In keeping with its motto, there is something "enchanting" about the way in which the "experience" of New Mexico tempts one into effusiveness (call it babbling if one chooses). New Mexico as place and as idea, as people and event, time and space is not easily translatable into words, be they arranged as history or story, the truth and distortions of fact or imagination, history or literature, or the data of the social sciences.

Because of this phenomenon, this influence of geography on literature and history, key works like Horgan's *Great River* and Harvey Fergusson's *Rio Grande* (1933) offer fine textual examples of history mingling with literature—more precisely of narrative history merging with historical fiction. Given later writers' preoccupation with the "New Journalism," with the "nonfiction novel," with what some critics have referred to as "faction," it might be argued that Horgan, and before him Fergusson, show us a way of writing history as narration infused with a sense of character, plot, dramatization, and setting (all of those techniques so closely associated with the novelist's art). It might be argued that they bequeath us an older way of writing history that is now thought of in some quarters, ironically, as "new."

It can be argued that Fergusson's *Rio Grande* influenced Horgan's *Great River*, at least indirectly. And the point could even be extended to say that Fergusson's *Rio Grande* probably influenced Horgan's other histories and biographies such as "About the Southwest: A Panorama of Nueva Granada," published in the *Southwest Review* in 1933, just two years after the first installment of *Rio Grande* appeared in *The American Mercury* in May 1931, as well as *From the Royal City* (1936), *The Centuries of Santa Fe* (1956), *Lamy of Santa Fe* (1975), and *Josiah Gregg and His Vision of the Early West* (1979).

Echoes of Harvey Fergusson's *Rio Grande* can also be heard in Erna Fergusson's books on New Mexico, including *Dancing Gods* (1931, although the influence here seems reciprocal), *Our Southwest* (1940), *Albuquerque* (1947), *Murder and Mystery in New Mexico* (1948), and *New Mexico: A Pageant of Three Peoples* (1951).

Moreover, Alice Corbin Henderson's *Brothers of Light* (1937), Laura Gilpin's *Rio Grande* (1949), even Tony Hillerman's *Rio Grande* (1975) and Robert Coles's *The Old Ones of New Mexico* (1973) all evidence some similarities to Fergusson's prototypic history of the Rio Grande.

More obviously, it should be said that the Rio Grande itself is the influence—and the "eyewitness," albeit ethnocentric, versions of it and New Mexico history that all these Anglo writers have encountered and recorded. (Any tracing of the ethnocentric Anglo assumptions of Charles F. Lummis, Harvey and Erna Fergusson, Witter Bynner, and Paul Horgan to the historiography of the recurrent frontier theories of Frederick Jackson Turner would take one too deeply into their respective biographies for consideration here.)

I have attempted to answer, in an essay published in *Southwest Review*, Frank D. Reeve's condemnation of *Great River* as history.[2] Reeve's carping "A Letter to Clio," published in the spring 1956 issue of *The New Mexico Historical Review*, reads now more like the result of vindictiveness than clear-headed judgment. Trying to sustain Stanley Walker's glibness, Reeve spoke directly to the muse of history, who presumably was in the habit of listening to him, and answered Walker's "Pretty, but is it history?" question straight out: "It is sometimes pretty, but it is not good history."[3] The debate about what makes "history" as well as what makes good history is, of course, still with us. But more and more the dichotomy suggested in Reeve's and Walker's either-or positioning of "prettiness" vs. history becomes, if not a false one, then certainly a misleading one.

In any event, I want to assert what might seem a truism: that history can be "pretty" and that the seemingly simple but actually very complex issue of reconciling these alleged polarities is part and parcel of the legacy of Fergusson's great book of history, biography, autobiography, interview, anecdote, memoir, and fiction, all published under the title of *Rio Grande*.

After the Fact: The Art of Historical Detection, a seminal book by James West Davidson and Mark Hamilton Lytle, provides a point of departure for such a consideration of *Rio Grande* as both pretty and history. In case anyone living in an age of the New History needs reminding, Davidson and Lytle remind us that history is more than traditional textbooks; "the explanations and interpretations 'behind' the story often turn out to be as interesting as the story itself."[4] In their essays Davidson and Lytle seek to counter what they see as excessive attempts by some historians to turn their discipline into "unadulterated social science." Too many historians, they think, have forgotten that

> history is rooted in the narrative tradition. As much
> as it seeks to generalize from past events, as do the
> sciences, it also remains dedicated to capturing the
> uniqueness of a situation. When historians neglect the
> literary aspect of their discipline—when they forget
> that good history begins with a good story—they risk
> losing the wider audience that all great historians have
> addressed. They end up, sadly, talking to themselves.[5]

Such a view of the narrative and populist roots of writing history suggests that Harvey Fergusson, more a humanistic than a scientific historian, was part of a much broader legacy, and that *Rio Grande* might best be considered as a trustee or guardian of an older and much larger tradition. That the tradition is also eclectic is significant, as is the belief that the process of writing history must be open to such eclecticism: "the use of pictorial evidence, questions of psychohistory, problems encountered analyzing oral interviews, the value of decision making models in political history, and so on."[6] Davidson and Lytle's definition of history seems to fit Harvey Fergusson's. In part, they define history this way—a definition that squares with Fergusson's statement in *Rio Grande*:

> History is not something that is simply brought out
> of the archives, dusted off, and displayed as "the way
> things really were." It is a painstaking construction,
> held together only with the help of assumptions, hy-
> potheses, and inferences.[7]

One can, of course, infer many of Fergusson's assumptions about history and the writing of it from the reading of *Rio Grande*. If one begins with the first chapter expecting fastidious documentation and acknowledgment of sources, maddening frustration immediately sets in. Horgan's *Great River* was severely criticized by Reeve, Walter Prescott Webb, and other academic historians for its lack of footnotes and vague attribution of sources. In part, this avoidance of footnotes on Horgan's part was responsible for his being regarded by some as an "amateur" historian. Seemingly, Horgan's choice not to footnote his sources is part of Fergusson's legacy. Fergusson uses no footnotes and for this reason, as well as more substantive ones, is clearly more the popularizer than the academician. It is interesting to mention in this context, by way of a small but significant digression, that only in the fourth edition of *Great River*, which appeared in the spring of 1985, does Horgan include Fergusson, as well as Bernard De Voto, in his bibliography. Horgan says, "Two works of distinction are absent from my bibliography. They were omitted not because they would have given me little, but because if I had reread them for the purposes of my study I feared that their persuasiveness in style and vision would have led me into unintended echoes in my own treatment of their subjects. These are *Rio Grande* by Harvey Fergusson (1933), a native New Mexican's superb account of life in the middle river valley of New Mexico, and *The Year of Decision* by Bernard De Voto (1943), a vivid recreation of the experience and impact of the War with Mexico."[8]

Fergusson was quite deliberate in his popularizer approach to New Mexico history. Advertisements for *Rio Grande* in *The American Mercury*, where it first appeared in installments, stress that its author is an unconventional historian—dealing with things that "conventional historians have generally neglected"—and that its author knew New Mexico as only a native son could: "He knows the Rio Grande country as few other men know it, and he makes its early heroes live again."[9] As for his manner of telling his story, it is characterized as full of "great skill and charm."[10]

When the reader finally comes to Fergusson's three and one-half pages of general bibliography, the reason for frustration with documentation is confirmed, for he states what the reader infers throughout the book. In Fergusson's words: "the veracity of the book is necessarily more psychological than factual. It is true only insofar as it is convincing."[11] Fergusson lists three major reasons for his less than meticulous documentation. First, he says the book is based as much on observation and interview as it is on documentary research "so that no complete accounting of its sources is possible." Second, "the book is an attempt at interpretation rather than a record," and third, he believes that "very little besides a few dates, names and statistics can be surely known about the past" (p. 293). Moreover, Fergusson asserts that, paradoxically, fiction is history and history is fiction. In his view, "a good realistic novel, it has been said, is history that might have happened, and the same is very largely true of a good history" (ibid.).

Having stated Fergusson's intentions and assumptions this broadly, let us now look a bit more specifically at the personae, the ethnocentric attitudes and values, the substantive and stylistic voices, and the architectonics of Fergusson as novelist-historian in *Rio Grande*. In a dozen chapters Fergusson begins with a description of the country, the land, and the river as they exist unto themselves, and then he moves swiftly to the intersection of the river with human history. He devotes one chapter to the Pueblo Indians (he names them more metaphorically and in echo of his sister, Erna, "the dancing builders"); two chapters to the Spanish "explorers" and "conquerors" by which designation he includes both Spanish soldiers and Franciscan clergy; one chapter to the Mexican-American "ricos" and "paisanos" of the lower and upper river valley (he labels them "the right people" and "the men of the soil," respectively); one chapter is allotted to the mountain men; another to the traders and "prairie" men like Josiah Gregg; one chapter to the "revolutionist," Manuel Armijo; one chapter to "the man of God," Lamy; one chapter to "longhorns and six shooters," which is devoted primarily to Elfego Baca; and a concluding chapter to "old town and new," a kind of generic, representative place caught up in the throes of welcoming the railroad, "progress," and its own future (clearly the town of Albuquerque).

Thus the body of the book is oriented toward history as biography, history as key individuals who, although representative of a type, also loomed larger than their type. The first and last chapters frame Fergusson's predilection for history as humanity by contrasting history as geography, flora, fauna—and as a town, as something man-made. Taken all in all, his scope is not really as large as the title of his book or his metaphorically comprehensive chapter titles would seem to suggest. By contrast, Horgan's canvas, upon which he paints his panorama of history and humanity along the Rio Grande, is much larger. He is decidedly right in observing that Fergusson's "'territory' of the R[io] G[rande] is very small compared to the whole course as treated in G[reat] R[iver]."[12] Just as apparent, however, is Horgan's tendency to write history as biography, to stress the difference that great people made on the great river.

It is also assumed in *Rio Grande*, in a kind of Turnerian "wave of the future" way, that it is inevitable (and appropriate) for American Indians to relinquish their world to the Spanish and for Spaniards to relinquish their dominion to Mexican Americans and subsequently Anglo Americans. Such assumptions, although seen as decidedly ethnocentric today, are presented in a kind of matter of fact, "that's just the way it was," historical scheme. The Indian is viewed as collective mind and motive with individualism and "democracy" appearing full blown only with the Anglo Americans—first with the mountain men and then the traders and, subsequently, the cowboys, outlaws, and rising middle class of western settlement. As William T. Pilkington says in his study of Fergusson, insofar as "the materials in *Rio Grande* are structured around a single paraphrasable theme," it is found in Fergusson's own statement, early in *Rio Grande*, that "the character of a country is the destiny of its people."[13]

What I have described as Fergusson's matter-of-fact acceptance of the coming of three different worldviews to the Rio Grande and their phased interaction with its geographical permanence, Pilkington sees as part of Fergusson's ambivalence toward the primitive and the modern. And James K. Folsom in his study of Fergusson, which chooses primarily to view *Rio Grande* as confirmation of Fergusson's understanding of southwestern history as utilized in his fiction, insists that "*Rio Grande* does not give a teleological view of history in which the past adds up to the glamorous present."[14] But there is evidence, particularly in Fergusson's sympathy for the mountain man as a harbinger of Anglo individualism and reckless progress; in Josiah Gregg as a man of action nicely balanced with the man of mind; and in the reckless courage of a folk-hero like Elfego Baca that Fergusson identified most closely with modern man and times. And although Horgan's historical heroes are generally military men—from Oñate to Stephen Watts Kearny to General Pershing—and priests, Horgan, too, was fascinated by the individualism of men like Josiah Gregg and the brand of Anglo-American progress that Gregg ushered in over the prairies and along the Santa Fe Trail. Nevertheless Archbishop Lamy remains the epitome of Horgan's heroes.

Insofar as Fergusson's ethnocentric assumptions about the primacy of

Anglo-American history are part of his legacy, *Rio Grande* can be read today as a controversial and racially divisive book. Maxwell Anderson, in an early response, accommodated Anglo-American encroachments into New Mexico this way:

> Something was lost here that will never be regained. Something is always lost when young barbarians trample the temples and relics of an older race, but since it was our culture that won we cannot bring ourselves to take the matter too much to heart. The lands of the earth, whether we like the code or not, belong to those who can take them.[15]

Arthur G. Pettit, writing thirty years later in the wake of the civil rights struggles of the 1960s, believes that Fergusson's "philosophical stance" in his historical novels was too severe, particularly in regard to the *ricos* and what Pettit calls the "fall of the New Mexican great house." Stopping short of labeling Fergusson's history "racist," Pettit offers a qualified concession and protest:

> It is certainly true that he [Fergusson] did not possess the deep sympathy for the New Mexican people that other (and lesser) Southwestern writers have displayed in recent years. Fergusson was concerned primarily with the special gifts of the Anglo-Saxon race as he saw them, and only secondarily with the defects of the New Mexican *ricos* as he saw them. . . . Nowhere in Fergusson's writing does he seem aware that when the Hispanos became Anglicized, they might—as they in fact did—compete on an equal basis with the Anglo-American.[16]

Compounding the legacy of Fergusson's ethnocentricity as a historian today is what can only be called his male chauvinism and his preoccupation with the alleged sexual predilections of Native American and Hispanic women for Anglo males. Cecil Robinson says, more or less in passing, that "Harvey Fergusson in his novels and in the cultural history *Rio Grande* has devoted a good deal of space to examining patterns of sexuality among the Mexican aristocrats of the Rio Grande valley during the period of the dominion of the big house."[17] But Fergusson's interest in what Robinson euphemistically calls "patterns of sexuality" accumulates to the point that the reader senses almost an obsession.

What begins, in the first instance, as a kind of anthropological exposition on "the masked dances of initiation and phallic worship" of the Pueblo Indians and what Fergusson calls their "grotesque humor of primitive eroticism" (p. 14) soon verges on outright titillation. Witness this account of Estevan's alleged appeal to native women: "There is a hint that Estevan had a way with the Indian women which was not altogether in accord with religious teachings and that the Friar [Marcos] thought he could expound salvation better while the negro was somewhere else" (p. 32). Also note this account of Estevan's acquisition of goods and concubines:

> At each village the people gave the negro food and shelter. From each village some of them followed him to the next. He soon found that they would deny him nothing he wanted and for the glory of God he began gathering up everything that looked valuable to him— chiefly turquoise and other semi-precious stones. Then he began also gathering women. These Mexican Indians are all polygamous and have never been celebrated for chastity so that perhaps it was not hard for Estevan to acquire concubines. Soon he was choosing the best-looking girls in every village and adding them to his retinue. (p. 35)

In his review of *Rio Grande* for the *Yale Review*, Horgan, who evidences similar ethnocentric assumptions about history in *Great River*, dwelt on the design of the book rather than its putative racism. He described this design as "a panorama of the different sorts of life that have been in the Southwest," but one that gains its focus and continuity not so much from changing cultural and temporal order but from the permanence of the land: "Change came so often in so short a period over the same land that the only stability is the land itself, which despite its seasonal furors, retains its constant quality, something challenging and wonderful to people's eyes, and something always impressive to their minds when they find out what sort of thing the land has known from previous peoples."[18]

Much of Fergusson's ethos as an Anglo observer and historian comes from his identification of himself as a New Mexico native, a person who experienced the old remnants of the history about which he writes and the newer inroads of Anglo-American progress everywhere about him. Thus there is a certain marginality about the way he dramatizes himself in *Rio Grande*. He frequently speaks of hiking and camping throughout the state; about the interviews he has conducted; about real and apocryphal anecdotes (many of them jokes and humorous accounts bordering on the tall tale). And he demonstrates, in tandem, his wide reading and research on New Mexico history. Furthermore, his authoritativeness with his *intended* audience is enhanced by his genealogy; by the at once disguised and announced fact that his father, H. B. Fergusson, who came as a southern gentleman and attorney to the rough and tough southern New Mexico mining town of White Oaks, made his way to Albuquerque and highly respectable marriage into the family of Franz Huning, an illustrious pioneer trader and settler in his own right and an individual with whom Harvey Fergusson identified much more than he did with his own father.

Many of the reviewers who first greeted *Rio Grande* recognized this authorial presence in the work and, in effect, hailed it as a kind of autobiography about growing up in an exotic and faraway land. This stylistic and rhetorical stance is underscored by Fergusson's writing to an apparently eastern audience by introducing them to a sort of strange and neglected part of their own American history.[19] Nowhere is this kind of "exoticism" better represented in *Rio Grande* than in Fergusson's rendering of his impressions of Penitente ritual. Lummis had preceded him in such ethnocentric portrayals, and Fergusson's pages on the Penitentes serve as representative of his methodology and persona as an Anglo native-son novelist-historian. An author who had climbed Wheeler Peak and Taos Mountain and found his way to sacred Blue Lake; gone swimming in the Rio Grande almost daily as a youth; hunted along its banks for waterfowl; fished it and its tributaries; boated down it—such an author, born to a state he had explored on his own, must be heeded by the uninitiated when he tells of his own experience with the secrets of "la Hermandad de los Penitentes."

Virtually all of one chapter, "The Men of the Soil," is devoted to the Penitentes. Fergusson begins by orienting the reader first to the highway between Taos and Santa Fe and then to a shorter, almost impassable road that cuts across the mountains and flattens out as it leads to the river through the villages of Chimayo, Cordova, Truchas, Trampas, Chamisal, and Peñasco—"each town with a singing name sits beside its singing water," as he phrases it. Here the men of the soil have settled. They are not regarded as "Americans" by Fergusson who says, ironically, that "few Americans have ever gained a foothold in this region" (p. 106), for it is viewed as a place and way of life out of a static, past century in New Mexico history. With the same kind of descriptive abilities he uses as a novelist, Fergusson sets the scene for his own mini-drama, his own personal intrusion into that time-frozen and idyllic spot of history. In his type of "socio-historical" account, setting and atmosphere are crucial. Here is part of his picturesque prose painting, his own version of "New Mexico baroque":

> Mountains shelter the past. In their arable crannies
> human life catches and clings like ore in the rock.
> Mountains check both expansion and invasion, the
> two great agents of change. . . . Most of the villages
> still are compact clusters of earthen houses, gathered
> together originally for protection, with their fields
> spread about them, the wooded mountains rolling up
> toward the peaks on one side, falling away to the river
> on the other. Almost every house has still its conical
> adobe oven outside the door and in the fall the walls
> are hung, as always, with scarlet strings of drying chile.
> The wide-hatted men and the black-shawled women
> are figures little changed. And here is an atmosphere,
> too, that belongs unmistakably to another age, before
> hurry began or machinery was invented. It is profoundly
> quiet but with a quiet that never seems dead. One gets
> from the faces and movements of the people and from
> their voices an impression of indolent vitality—of life
> that is never driven or frantic as it is wherever machines
> set the pace and the hope of progress an ever-receding
> goal [sic]. (p. 107)[20]

Musing about the historical significance of such people, Fergusson identifies them as the only true peasants within the borders of the United States, people in whom—as he describes it—"the blood of an ancient European peasantry mingles with that of sedentary Indians." And he contrasts them with Anglo-Saxon men who as wanderers and exploiters have always "despised" people like these who draw their very identity from their closeness with the soil. But Fergusson speculates that the whole future of all Latin America belongs to these "men of the soil." It is in such an interpretation that Fergusson's "ambivalence" toward Anglo-American progress is sensed even though the reader knows, on balance, Fergusson approves and is a part of that Anglo-American progress that, by implication, might one day collide with the endurance of the Latin American peasantry.

Relying on the accounts of Josiah Gregg, James W. Abert, and Frank M. Edwards, who was one of Kearny's volunteers, Fergusson outlines the corruption among the priesthood during "that dark period after the pioneering Franciscan friars had left and before the reforms of Bishop Lamy . . ." (p. 110). The "men of the soil" were forced by the unwar-

ranted demands and outright exploitation by the priesthood and the *ricos*
to live as they could, at times outside the laws of both the church and ex-
isting government. Thus Penitente ritualized flagellation, outside the sanc-
tion of the church, is explained by Fergusson as a natural response to a
more worldly persecution: "Overtaxed by the padres he [the Penitente/
paisano] dispensed with their services when he could not afford them,
keeping still intact his own faith, which was always a graft of Catholic
dogma and ritual upon a primitive idolatry and drew its strength more
from earth then from heaven" (p. 113).

Fergusson continues to build to his own Anglo experience with Penitente ritual through several paragraphs contrasting Anglo and Hispanic
food and entertainment and, again, "sexual patterns," all of which today
seems irksome and ethnocentric. The *paisano*'s is considered a culture of
others—much different than that of the Anglo historian and his Anglo
audience. Note this instance of editorializing on Fergusson's part:

> All Latin-Americans love ceremony and ritual and
> among them the established forms of human conduct
> seem never to go dead as they do among us where for-
> mality is almost a synonym for dullness and sponta-
> neous joy in generally a violent smashing of traditional
> restraints. (p. 114)

Or take this sweeping generalization: "It is an apparent contradiction
in the character of the common Mexican that he may be the most proudly
independent of men or the most servile" (p. 115). Caught up in what seems
not only biased but totally digressive commentary, Fergusson continues
to make ethnocentric if not racist pronouncements disguised as general-
ized truths about so-called Mexican and American relations in the 1930s:

> Unless he has been too much corrupted by contact
> with the Americanos he will often refuse payment for
> his hospitality though nothing [*sic*] averse to accepting
> suitable gifts. But if you hire a Mexican to work for
> you he is likely to regard you as a potential source of
> all things needed and to become a somewhat importu-
> nate solicitor of favors. Give him half a chance and he
> will get himself into your debt and stay there. In a
> word, he will relapse into peonage. . . . Both political
> and economic life in New Mexico still suffer from his
> instinctive love of a feudal relationship to some leader.
> (p. 116)

Needless to say, such speculation is part of a legacy of historical inter-pretation rightfully discounted today. Today, a more congenial interpre-tation of the Penitente brotherhood is that of Sabine R. Ulibarrí who, in his wonderfully entertaining and enlightening *cuentos* of northern New Mexico, writes with pride about the character and contribution of his people:

> Now older and wiser, I contemplate the panorama of
> the past in astonishment and I can see the tremendous
> importance that the presence of the Penitentes had on
> the history of our people. If we pull them out, forget or
> ignore the Penitentes, the historical picture of New
> Mexico crumbles.[21]

This is not to say that Fergusson fails to recognize the Penitentes as sig-nificant in New Mexico history. His appraisal is not as categorically pos-itive as Ulibarrí's. For Fergusson, theirs was a faith that allowed "New Mexicans [to remain] devout while the priests robbed them of the rites of marriage, of baptism and even of burial from the Church." In all, the Pen-itente brotherhood, according to Fergusson, "was the flower of a spiri-tual integrity which had its roots, lower and deeper than those of any church, in an ancient sacrifice of blood, in the ecstatic acceptance of pain and death" (p. 118).

One recent commentator believes that "the 'darker' impression of the morada chapels is best expressed by Harvey Fergusson in *Rio Grande*."[22] Insofar as this is true it is partly attributable to the perspective of wonder and fear occasioned by childhood. For it is from the point of view of a child's memories recounted that Fergusson dramatizes his eyewitness ac-count of Penitente ritual.

Fergusson first saw the Penitentes in 1903 when he was thirteen. And he testifies that it is from a "pop-eyed" account that he went home to write immediately after the experience that he says he "paraphrases" in *Rio Grande*. It is an account not unlike his sister's account of the Zuni Shalako ceremony in its compelling, albeit ethnocentrically envisioned, power. All in all, it has the flavor of a boyhood trip into the past, the log of a mysterious "time-machine" traveler. As such, he indulges his novel-istic flair, stressing his physical sensations, the response of his body, like the Penitentes, to pleasure and pain:

> What I remember best is the all-night ride in the bitter
> March weather with freezing hands and feet. The wind
> had piled tumble weeds along the road and every few

miles we would touch a match to a pile of these and
warm ourselves at a brief flare that lit the mountains,
still patched with snow, and made a dance of shadows
among cedar brush and boulders. I remember dawn-
light shining on an adobe town and a breakfast of
crackers and cheese in a little store and then excited
Mexicans coming to tell that the Penitentes were
marching to the graveyard. (p. 120)

Having traveled with what he calls "penitente-hunters," tourists in
search of alien sights, Fergusson spends three full pages describing the
naked and gashed backs of the twelve men who whipped and chanted
their way, covered with blood to their very heels, down a hill to a small
graveyard where they knelt before a wooden cross, and then returned,
marching in slow order, to the tempo of their own blood-drenched whips
back up the hill to their morada. Fergusson, bareheaded (in contrast to
the black-capped Penitentes), along with his eager companions—four or
five other boys—followed the procession up the hill and entered the
chapel. What he saw would rivet the attention of any boy:

The smoky lantern hung from the middle of the roof
and two candles lit an altar at the far end. It was
draped and curtained in black and a human skull occupied its very center. Not the cross, but a skull and
cross bones were embroidered or painted in white on
the black altar cloth. (p. 121)

It was a shrine of death, heightened in its horror for him because of the
secret room at the back of the chapel where no one but members could
enter. But Fergusson says he was close enough to touch "the bloody flesh
of their backs" (p. 121). The small black figure before the altar became
animated, transformed before his very eyes, and ghostlike, "rose and became a man, certainly less than five feet tall, in a black robe with a horse-
hair rope about his middle" (p. 121). Fergusson reports that the small
man (almost a creature of unearthly dimension in the description) spoke
briefly in Spanish, after which all the Penitentes filed out of the chapel
and began their reenactment of the ascent to Calvary. In that pageantry,
which Fergusson typifies as the death of Christ "amid pandemonium and
lamentation," is found the dramatic climax not just to the ceremony but
the author's description of it, for in one action-filled, frenetic paragraph
the startled and agonizing motion and sound of mock crucifixion is presented. That one scene is a masterwork of the convergence of character,

plot, and setting—the fictions, if you will—of a historian. Never content merely to describe and always seeking to reconcile his own experiences with larger more philosophical interpretations, Fergusson draws his own allegorical meanings from his encounter with the Penitente brotherhood. What he saw as alien to his own Anglo youth and culture he attempts to synthesize, to universalize. And whether one agrees with his conclusions, whether one sees his descriptions as truthful or distorted (as most perceptions are), the reader must applaud Fergusson's reverence—and that is not too great a word in context—for the lessons of history, and the overall legacy of New Mexico and the Rio Grande, which tends to function, ultimately, as a metaphor, not merely for New Mexico but for the larger Southwest. Nowhere is Fergusson more incisive than in a conclusion such as this:

> The Penitentes were only a delightful horror then. It is
> the diversities of life that strike us first. Time reveals
> the unities, bringing a sort of comprehension for any-
> thing men may do. Those whips laid on bloody backs
> now seem only a brutal and forthright form of the
> discipline which every man must lay upon himself—
> symbols of the guilt and fear which are the penalties
> of human consciousness. (p. 123)

If this is an example of what a reader like Stanley Walker objects to as the babbling to which New Mexico writers succumb when struck by the fever of "New Mexico baroque," then Harvey Fergusson, like his sister Erna, is guilty of nothing more than trying to express in language what is finally inexpressible. There is, admittedly, much in *Rio Grande* that has the ring of sound lacking sense; passages, pages, even chapters, that might well be assessed as "pretty" but not "good history." And if *Rio Grande*'s final legacy is an ethnocentric one that seems flawed to the point of embarrassment and boorishness, one need only ponder what our conception of New Mexico's past and our larger national and human pasts would be if not written as they were seen, cultural biases notwithstanding. In *Rio Grande* as in his other works of history and fiction, Harvey Fergusson wrote from his heart and his mind the best he could about a process and a place so wondrous, so spectacular as to provide a continuing legacy for us all.

WITTER BYNNER, POET IN ADOBIA

In other words, it's a busy life but not a happy one. I long to be back in adobia.
—WITTER BYNNER TO WILLARD JOHNSON, DECEMBER 31, 1923

Witter Bynner arrived in Santa Fe in 1922. He was forty-one and much recognized as an editor, poet, and lecturer. Born in Brooklyn, New York, in 1881, he grew up in Brookline, Massachusetts, was graduated (with honors) from Harvard in 1902, and served as an editor at *McClure's* from 1902 to 1906. Bynner's editor and biographer, James Kraft, says about Bynner's beginnings, "It was the older New England as it existed in late-nineteenth-century Boston that most firmly shaped his life."[1] This is, no doubt, true—since artists are mostly formed by the places and impressions of youth—but Bynner's trip to China in 1917, resulting in the publication of his translations of Chinese poetry, *The Jade Mountain*, in 1929, greatly influenced his manner and reputation as a poet, as did his time teaching in California at Berkeley. However, his various trips to Mexico and the Southwest resulted in another significant Bynner book, also published in 1929 (with a second printing in 1930), called *Indian Earth*.

By the time of his death in Santa Fe in 1968, at the age of eighty-six, Bynner had been involved in festivals, a great literary hoax, and political lobbying efforts (he opposed Bronson Cutting for the state legislature in 1926 and later was encouraged by Cutting to run for governor). He had been portrayed in fiction by such dissimilar novelists as D. H. Lawrence and Harvey Fergusson and was known as one of Santa Fe's most famous poets and one of the Southwest's most colorful artistic personalities. His biography, art, and legend are inextricably linked to Santa Fe and the Southwest—to the region he referred to as "adobia" in a jazzy letter of New Year's Eve 1923 to his student, secretary, traveling companion, friend, and editor of *Laughing Horse*, Willard "Spud" Johnson, a letter in which he expresses his satiety with New York and his homesickness for New Mexico shortly after first discovering it (*SL*, p. 109).

How adobia affected Bynner as artist and citizen and how he, in turn, influenced the society, individuals, and issues of his time are significant topics in the cultural and literary history of Santa Fe, New Mexico, and the larger Southwest. Bynner's essays about Santa Fe and about Native American culture and ceremony afford interesting insights into Anglo-American/Native American acculturation and accommodation in the Southwest, as do his "Pueblo Dances" poems found in *Indian Earth*.[2]

Bynner was a focal point for the Santa Fe art colony—as party giver, an impresario for the talent of peers and initiates, and as an advocate for indigenous, especially Native American civil and cultural rights—and for women's suffrage. Associated closely in his early Santa Fe days with Alice Corbin Henderson, D. H. and Frieda Lawrence, Spud Johnson, Paul Horgan, Robert Hunt, Mabel and Tony Luhan, Haniel Long, Lynn Riggs, Mary Austin, and numerous others, Bynner outlived most of the local writers and luminaries of his era, even fellow poet Winfield Townley Scott, who died only months before Bynner, and Oliver La Farge, who died five years earlier. In its obituary of Bynner, *The Santa Fe New Mexican* described the passing of that "triumvirate of great writers" as the end of an era.[3] Scott had called Bynner "one of Santa Fe's most distinguished residents" and La Farge, in 1956, had praised him as a giant, a man "who stands so tall that he can be seen from wherever men read English" (*SFNM*, June 2, 1968).[4]

There was always much reciprocal back-patting among the Santa Fe artist colony. Paul Horgan, who served for a summer as Bynner's secretary, and who introduced Bynner to Robert Hunt (Bynner's lifelong friend, and editor of his *Selected Poems* [1943]), preferred, ultimately, to stay in Roswell when "some of the individuals who were locally called 'sensitives' began to seem somewhat grotesque, self-advertising, and responsive to opportunities for envy and competition."[5] These sentiments notwithstanding, Horgan, in the finest critical appraisal of Bynner's writing by a friend, isolates Bynner's frank and democratic qualities as a poet—one capable of much "technical loveliness."[6]

At the invitation of Alice Corbin Henderson—an associate editor for *Poetry: A Magazine of Modern Verse*—Bynner first traveled to Santa Fe to lecture on his China travels and to read Chinese poetry.[7] Santa Fe had a population of a little more than 7,236 when Bynner arrived and the city was beginning to gain reputation for its high, healing mountain air for pulmonary and tuberculosis patients.[8] An illness, probably the flu, extended his lecture visit and he took a room at the Sunmount Sanitorium, which, due to a shortage of hotels, also accommodated travelers. Alice

Corbin, her artist/architect husband, William Penhallow Henderson, and their daughter, Alice Henderson ("Little Alice," as Bynner and others called her), hospitably entertained Bynner and took him to see his first Pueblo dances (Bullock, p. 1).

Bynner soon rented a three-room adobe house, at 342 Buena Vista, belonging to Paul Burlin, which Bynner later purchased and turned into a rambling "show-case" hacienda. Over the ensuing years, Bynner reciprocated his own agog brand of the Henderson hospitality to hundreds of guests. The impressions recorded at his first Pueblo dances are turned to great effect in his most famous American Indian poem, "A Dance for Rain (Cochiti)," and in the other "Pueblo Dances" poems collected in *Indian Earth*. Seldom noticed today, these poems represent the best poetic account of Bynner's feelings for adobia and the Southwest. In his editor's foreword to the 1943 edition of *Selected Poems*, Robert Hunt says about these poems,

> [The] poems on the Pueblo dances of New Mexico and
> Arizona, are in no sense the hasty expressions of the
> casual or passing admirer of the Southwest scene or its
> Indian dances; they are the considered result of acutely
> sympathetic understanding and familiarity with such
> ceremonies over a period of many years.[9]

Ostensibly, the entire grouping was completed within seven or so years of Bynner's first viewing of Pueblo dances with the Hendersons. The point of view, assumptions, and techniques of Bynner's Pueblo poems must be placed in the context of his China experience and his arrival in Santa Fe in the early 1920s as an eastern tourist turned fiercely loyal settler in, and nativistic champion of "adobia."

In 1924, three years after coming to Santa Fe, Bynner wrote an essay for Willard Johnson's irreverent publishing venture, *Laughing Horse*, ambivalently chastising and celebrating Santa Fe as "A City of Change." For the most part, he was thankful that he had come in time. Here is part of his description of what he first found, enthralled, at his and the ancient city's intersection in history:

> To be sure, the great oblong Plaza reaching the Cathe-
> dral had long since been cut in twain: half of it, the
> Cathedral end, solidified now into a Grecian bank, a
> Middle West department store and a New Mexican
> post office. On three sides of the surviving plaza were
> the usual haphazard and hideous fronts of an American

business street, but on the fourth side the old Gover-
nors' Palace, massive adobes, seasoned pillars and *vigas*
still held its ground; its *portales*, like a public cloister,
still shaded one sidewalk, as they had formerly and
properly shaded all four; and its *patio* was still a garden-
spot with trees. On Sunday evenings when the band
played, youths would stream in one direction round
the Plaza and in the opposite directions maidens, just
apart from one another and just as aware of one another as I have seen them in Mexican cities. Older
women moved nun-like, on Sundays or weekdays, with
soft black shawls over their heads, the fringe hanging
down their dresses. Burros came daily in droves with
round burdens of firewood, or bumped lazily from a
jiggling trot. Though there was no longer an open
market in the Plaza, there was one street left where
wagons, from ranches or from Indian villages, held
corn, tomatoes, apples, melons, and other fresh produce to be bought directly from the dark-eyed
drivers. . . . On the outlying hills were venturous
artists in sombreros, corduroys, and bright necker-
chiefs. When Holy Days came, there were bonfires
and the Virgin or St. Francis was carried through the
streets by walking worshippers. And round about the
landscape, in their snug, earthen pueblos, were Indians,
guarding the dignity of their race and instinctively
living the beauty of their religion and their art, as they
had been doing for hundreds of years. I had come in
time.[10]

These rather romanticized, nostalgic perceptions of an outsider, recollected in as short a time of historical process as four years, are not the
impressions and yearnings of a perennial tourist. Bynner was so taken
with what he had discovered, before the ravages of modernity and
progress set in, that he settled in "adobia."

Soon [he says] I had found my own adobe, one of the
oldest, with a broad-beamed roof to shed homely dirt
on me in windy weather and primitive rain in wet. I
was above the troubled world. I was washed clean of
the war, I was given communion each night when sun-
set would elevate the hosts on the Sangre de Cristo

mountains. I was writing to friends who lived on another planet. I had found something not to be found
elsewhere in These States, a town too much itself to
be feverishly imitating its neighbors. Nothing strained,
nothing silly, just an honest-to-God town, seasoned
and simple, easily breathing its high air. ("A City of
Change," *PP*, p. 46)

Adobia, however, was a city of American "discontent," and it continued to pay the price of Americanized progress—as Bynner well recognizes,
laments, but also accepts: "The streets which were rough and made us go
slowly are smooth now and make us go fast. The native earth which used
to touch our feet on the edge of the Plaza is being sealed out of sight, out
of touch. These pavements may grow machines now, but not persons. The
little adobe houses near the Plaza have cast down their grassy crowns before a bulk of garages in Santa Fe style, yes, but inviting blatant vehicles
which hurry people's errands and harden their faces" (ibid., pp. 46–47).

As early as 1924, Bynner acknowledges his own participation in a
deadly process of stylizing and advertising a city that was initially naively
oblivious to its own identifying uniqueness:

We are all doing it. We cannot help ourselves. We are
attracting people here. We are advertising. We are
boosting. We cannot care enough that, by professional-
izing the apparent difference of Santa Fe, we are killing
the real difference. We are crowding out the natives, to
make room for improved houses with artificial warp-
ings. We are changing our town from the city different
to the city indifferent. Even the Indians are feeling us,
are yielding to us. Being Americans, we have to man-
age our neighbors. And it is always for their good. A
few years ago, the Pueblos conducted their own delib-
erations and maintained their own character. Because
of their simplicity, they were threatened with unjust
loss of their lands. Not only Santa Fe but the country
at large came to their rescue, spurring Congress to pass
at last needful legislation. As to their lands, the Pueblos
are much better off than they were a few years ago; but
almost any month now, a non-Indian with a childlike
face and a flowing tie may be found steamrolling an
Inter-Pueblo Council according to his whim and writing letters for them in imitation Indian. . . . And what

shall it profit the Pueblos to win their land if they lose
their way. (ibid., pp. 47–48)

Bynner's protest, and acceptance, of change—echoing the satirical
spirit of his friend Johnson's *Laughing Horse*—is mitigated by his appreciation, his jubilation in the vitality of the laminating and interchanging
cross-cultural process then (and increasingly still) shaping Santa Fe,
changing the land of adobes into the more glib, hip, jazz-age conjurings
and connotations of "adobia" (for example, as Bynner only half sarcasti-
cally quips, "Why had those dance faith who had rather dance jazz"
[ibid., p. 49]). If the Pueblos have, in their dances before Catholic churches,
added "an older beauty to the beauty of the saints," might not those
dances, and their spirit, be integrated into Santa Fe as town?

It is this spirit of ultimate integration and reconciliation of diverse perceptions, beliefs, and "styles" that infuses the "Pueblo Dances" poems in
Indian Earth. For in those poems Bynner presumes to record and report
the impressions of a persona now Anglo American, and then Native
American, of observer and observed, the "I" as voyeur "other" become
participant, Anglo poet imaginatively touching the Indian earth. In a
piece of tourism written in 1928 for the passenger department of the
Atchison, Topeka, and Santa Fe Railroad, Bynner expresses his empathic
attitude toward Native American dance (an attitude that informs his
Pueblo Dances poems): "Only by watching them in their own spirit, may
any one of us deserve to see them" ("Pueblo Dances," *PP*, p. 329).

Bynner's attempts to see and render Pueblo dances in the spirit of the
native dancers themselves are colored by his year in China, his empathy,
too, for the "heart of China": "It sometimes seems as if these people, in
their heightened moments had cherished alive through the centuries the
Taoist wisdom of Laotzu and as if their dances were an outward and still
visible sign of his inward invisible grace" (ibid., p. 330). Paul Horgan em-
phasized this Asian/American Indian correspondence in his account of
Bynner's collection of Chinese art, donated to the Roswell Museum in
1954:

> The Bynner Collection . . . [provides] materials for
> study and enlightenment in one of the largest themes in
> American history—a theme that is in both the most an-
> cient and the most immediate senses historically local
> to New Mexico. This is the theme of the colonization
> of western North American from Asia, many thou-
> sands of years ago, when the ancestors of our Indians
> came across the Bering Sea, bringing the orient to our

hemisphere. Aside from scientific evidence for this theory, now generally accepted, there is evidence in the arts and crafts of today's New Mexico Indians that their works and those of the Chinese orient have common seeds. To illustrate this tremendous idea that Museum will be able to present Chinese examples from the Bynner Collection alongside examples of Pueblo and other Indian cultures to show our people today how the oldest links can be matched with some of the newest in the chain of events that brought human life to our part of the world. This ability to tell something of the earliest chapter of our life story in the southwest represents a great educational resource for the Museum in all its related fields of history and archeology and art, and it comes to us only through Mr. Bynner's splendid gift.[11]

Elsewhere Horgan, in his critical assessment of Bynner's development as a poet, sees the Pueblo Dances poems in *Indian Earth* (he calls them a suite) and the Southwest "adobia" ambiance of place that surrounds them as a kind of bridge, not just between China and the New World, but between Bynner's early and late phases, his youth and his maturity:

[The Pueblos] moved him to answer them, and various of the opinions in his own soul. The Indian fatalism was impressive for its dignity, its complete innocence of any such reassuring optimism, or need of it, as lay at the heart of lyric democracy. To the Indians, things were neither all right nor all wrong with the world. Things were as they were. It was enough to recognize that and make the world with the stuff of every day. It could be made and beautifully integrated, as the Indian pueblo community showed. It could so find a mysteriously powerful relationship between people and the environment. I believe (since the poet's organism, aeolian by tradition, responds to all the winds that blow over it) that Bynner, in the Southwest, found some modification, some handsome compromise in awareness and admission possible between the ecstatic optimism of his youth and the tragic strength of his maturity as a poet. ("CE," p. 292)

This process of modification and maturation afforded Bynner by the larger Southwest, Horgan surmises, resembles the quality John Keats found so essential to all poets, and so prevalent in Shakespeare—that is, the quality of "Negative Capability," the capacity "of being in uncertainties, mysteries, doubts, without any irritable reaching after fact and reason."[12] Bynner's development as a poet in adobia, then, was tempered and directed by his Southwest sojourn, contributing to the modification and conditioning of a man/poet brought to life's terms—

> for his vision was sharpening all the time and his fight
> growing more and more articulate so that short of
> dying or never sobering up from the poet's afflatulent
> intoxication, he must undergo conversion from the
> optimisms of youth; from the evasions of wit; from
> dreams of the future; from pinching his friends; and
> resolve, if he could, the tragical variety of the artist's
> nature with the harmony of comprehension and admis-
> sion; something like the instinctive creature wisdom of
> the Indians, who looked upon themselves as beings in
> a world both warm and fecund and sere and barren.
> ("CE," p. 293)

Such an accounting goes beyond stereotypical Native American stoicism to mythic harmony with geographical place and cosmic heaven, person as human, as dancer, and as deity. Not entirely coincidentally, such theorizing about Bynner's progress as a poet was undergirded by the obvious fact that Bynner's arrival at middle age converged with his arrival in adobia. Even so, it is a pervasive acceptance in all of Bynner's southwestern writings and Pueblo poems, during the 1920s especially. Such was his acceptance of the vitality of Santa Fe as a city of change. Such was his awe at the vitality witnessed, and felt, in the Pueblo dances that he attempted to represent in verse.

Of the six Pueblo Dance poems in *Indian Earth*, "A Dance for Rain (Cochiti)" is characteristic. It was "A Dance for Rain (Cochiti)" that Bynner himself ironically read (along with his favorite poem, "Epithalamium and Elegy")—through the technological magic of tape recording—at his own funeral.[13] The witticism so closely associated with Bynner's personality, and airily reflected in the quote, "If Witter come, can spring be far behind," is nowhere more seriously and beautifully said than in one of Bynner's best lines (from "Epithalamium and Elegy")—and a condensed credo it is, simultaneously appropriate to ceremonies of marriage and death: "My single constancy [Bynner avows] is love of life."[14]

That energetic love of life, as prayer for life, permeates "A Dance for Rain (Cochiti)." In the poem life is at once deified and made tangible, a god persons could taste and hold in their hands, "a god that you could see, / Rain, rain, in Cochiti."[15] The metamorphosis from cloudless sky to rain cloud and following rain—all conjured up by the feathered and furred and garlanded Cochiti dancers—is matched by the metamorphosis in the poet/speaker who marks his observance of the evocation as a watershed in his own life, one that he recommends to the reader:

> *You may never see rain, unless you see*
> *A dance for rain at Cochiti,*
> *Never hear thunder in the air*
> *Unless you hear the thunder there,*
> *Nor know the lightning in the sky*
> *If there's no pole to know it by.*
> *They dipped the pole just as I came,*
> *And I can never be the same*
> *Since those feathers gave my brow*
> *The touch of wind that's on it now,*
> *Bringing over the arid lands*
> *Butterfly gestures from Hopi hands*
> *And holding me, till earth shall fail,*
> *As close to earth as a fox's tail. (IE, p. 63)*

What the dance substantiates for the poet/speaker is "That death is weak and life is strong," as he describes the ceremonial dress of fox skin and turtle rattle and sprays of pine and the "windy line" and "creeping tread" and the "heart . . . beating in the drum." In the dramatizations of the dance the ghosts of the dead are raised and ministered to by the rain, when it comes, so as "to make core and children go" (ibid., p. 64). With the coming of the rain, so too comes the climax of the poem:

> *The rain made many suns to shine,*
> *Golden bodies in a line*
> *With leaping feather and swaying pine.*
> *And the brighter the bodies, the brighter the rain*
> *Where thunder heaped it on the plain.*
> *Arroyos had been empty, dry,*
> *But now were running with the sky;*
> *And the dancers' feet were in a lake,*
> *Dancing for the people's sake. (ibid., p. 65)*

And in "A Buffalo Dance (Santo Domingo)" the poet/speaker merges completely with the people, with the indigenous dancers, just as they have merged with the animals whose lives they are acting out, so that the poet/observer merges, too, with the earth itself:

And a larger earth
Absolved us
Of ourselves
With a song of ourselves,
Of godly animals.
Of godly men
Who forever follow
The rising and the falling of the hills,
Deer, buffalo, elk, antelope, hunter,
Our thighs and ankles painted with the red adobe and
    white rain,
Our breast and forehead with the turquoise sky.
(ibid., p. 71)

Certainly such a metaphorical merger with the red adobe, the white rain, and the turquoise sky, offers more than a poetic epiphany. In all of *Indian Earth*, but especially in "A Dance for Rain (Cochiti)" and "A Buffalo Dance (Santo Domingo)," is seen the epitome of Bynner's heartfelt and soulful longing for the elements, the colors, the textures, the social, cultural, and racial vitality of all that the Southwest meant to him as a person who, as he declared to his friend Spud Johnson, longed more for a happy life in New Mexico than a busy one in New York (or California), longed as a man and as a poet to be in Mexico, or in China transposed—in Santa Fe, in the Southwest, in "adobia."

PART
TWO

INDIAN VOICES

INTRODUCTION

It is by now well established that N. Scott Momaday's *House Made of Dawn* (1968) won more than a Pulitzer Prize. It won the way for a re-awakening of American Indian literature, particularly the novel. Momaday's voice, more ancient than modern, struck a modern nerve in critics who had not yet discovered the connections between the primitive, the indigenous and the aboriginal, the modern and the sophisticated.

Momaday had his indigenous as well as Anglo-European predecessors, it was soon realized, as did all of "American" literature, reaching back thirty thousand years or more into the pre-Columbian oral, aboriginal, mythic, and legendary "literary" past. Momaday's work, however, opened up new pathways of recognition for forerunners such as D'Arcy McNickle, and the many "Indian voices" before and contemporary with him. And in the wake of such a new/old Native American presence came a whole new "school" of American Indian novelists and poets, new keepers of the sacred word, protectors of Indian presence, pride, and protest.

Soon it became apparent too that although these writers were Indian in heritage and theme, they were also universal. If they were Indian writers, they were simultaneously American writers, and, even more generally, writers transcending labels categorizing them as "Native American" or Indian.

James Welch and Ray Anthony Young Bear were and still are among the best of this best new bunch of writers. My initial interest in them resided partly in the fact that I knew them, and their literary talents increased all the more in my eyes because of our relative familiarity. But my interest in their work was heightened and sustained because of its quality. Their writings wore well and soon gained enough momentum to secure them a kind of anti-canonized "classic" status.

Young Bear I first met and came to know when he was a young poet enrolled at the University of Northern Iowa where I was on the faculty.

He lived nearby on the Mesquakie Settlement west of Tama and, learning of his fine poems in *The American Poetry Review* and other smaller literary journals, I soon enticed him to speak to some of my classes in Native American literature. Soon, but only for a brief time of a semester or so, he enrolled in an independent study course with me and subsequently submitted several of his poems as part of an "imaginative" writing project. Since he lived the literature which my students and I were then merely studying, he needed not so much a critical as a creative opportunity for expression. Professor become once again student!

Welch came to Northern Iowa at my invitation and read from a work then in progress, a novel later published as *The Death of Jim Loney* (1979). It was powerful stuff and Welch's strong voice and flint-honed style were much belied by his youthful, clean-cut, blue-blazer, checked-sport-shirt, horn-rim glasses look. In his more sedate, refined way, he was as angry and as rebellious as Young Bear. And listening to them both converse, over beer and *hors d'oeuvres*, about their developing careers as writers spurred newly stirring desires to do some imaginative writing myself and to secure my own Indian, mixed-blood ancestral moorings.

Like many reader-critics, in analyzing and in listening to the profound artistry of Welch and Young Bear I heard not just my country's mixed pride and guilt about its wrongful disregard for indigenous peoples but also my own heart's rhythmic and rejuvenated indigenous yearnings.

In the Indian voices and voicings of James Welch's Blackfeet/Gros Ventre and Ray Anthony Young Bear's Mesquakie heritages I came into fuller respect for and understanding of my own Cherokee cultural legacies. Their voices, blending with the Anglo vistas of Lummis, the Fergussons, and Bynner, were an integral part of what I heard and saw as a native son of New Mexico and the American West. These Indian voices still speak, strong, and with much medicine of the *word*.

THE WORD MEDICINE OF JAMES WELCH

WINTER IN THE BLOOD

Much of the tragicomic effect of James Welch's masterful first novel, *Winter in the Blood* (1974), depends on the elements of mystery and mock intrigue and their thematic and structural interplay.[1] Although mystery and mock intrigue are identifiable as distinct and separate elements throughout the novel, they are nevertheless organically related, not only to each other but to the central metaphor of the book and all of its accompanying imagery—the pervasive notion of "winter in the blood."

Precisely because Welch's book is so organic, mystery and mock intrigue are cornerstones in his construction of point of view and method of narration; in advancing the plot; in the sense of setting the atmosphere of "Big Sky" Montana; and in overall theme and imagery—the anatomy of the language itself.

Without attempting an exhaustive analysis of the ways in which all of these aspects of *Winter in the Blood* relate to each other, I seek merely to illustrate partially how mystery and mock intrigue work together in the composition of this fascinating novel. I do not mean to suggest that such a consideration is the only way to approach the novel. Welch's artistry is too richly complex for that. But a consideration of mystery and mock intrigue provides a way of synthesizing views that see the novel as either tragic or comic; as either a Native American or a nonethnic book; as either a modern psychological novel or a Western; as either regional or universal— as either one thing or the other.

Neither do I mean by the use of the terms *mystery* and *mock intrigue* that *Winter in the Blood* is limited to being a full-fledged mystery novel; nor that it is an open-throttled, no-holds-barred parody of the spy novel or the novel of intrigue. The terms *mystery* and *mock intrigue* are intended more broadly than that for purposes of the present discussion. In such a context, *Winter in the Blood* is viewed as only a partial parody of the spy novel. Simultaneously, *Winter in the Blood* may be read as having certain characteristics (certainly not all) of the mystery or detective novel. There are, to be sure, many minor "crimes" and at least two major mysterious deaths to solve (call them "murders" or, more specifically, suicide and manslaughter?) This is to say that in terms of literary genre and mode, *Winter in the Blood* is no one, single thing. It is a realistic novel, a surrealist poem, an absurdist drama, a picaresque mock-epic adventure, a sociological satire on American Indian and non-Indian relations, a modern, "adult" Western—in short, *Winter in the Blood* defies easy classification. Because of its kaleidoscopic nature, the novel invites broad definitions and merged definitions. And that is why mystery and mock intrigue are intended broadly here.

All three traditional definitions of mystery apply: (1) anything that arouses curiosity because it is unexplained, inexplicable, or secret; (2) the quality of being inexplicable or secret; and (3) a piece of fiction dealing with a puzzling crime. Intrigue may be defined as (1) a covert or underhanded scheme; (2) the use of such schemes or to engage in them; (3) a clandestine love affair; (4) suspense and mystery. Mock intrigue, then, is, as might be expected, the mocking of intrigue and its associated narrative conventions for humorous and satirical ends—or even, as in the case of *Winter in the Blood*, the ends of tragedy and pathos.[2]

There is, admittedly, a certain redundancy in the use of the two terms together insofar as "mystery" suggests intrigue, and "intrigue" in turn suggests "mystery." This redundancy is compounded in that the interplay of these elements in the novel first expand and then contract—are, in terms of fictive spatial form, expansive and reflexive. In the broadest architectonic terms I equate "mystery" with the more serious, profoundly tragic ideas and events and feelings (or in this instance, lack of feelings) which cluster around the narrator and his center of consciousness (benumbed and awakened, "distanced" and "immediate"; that is, the "blood consciousness," as it were, that comes from within the narrator and is associated with the book's title and controlling metaphor, and is evoked in its numerous "objective correlatives," to call upon T. S. Eliot's terminology). Also, in an architectonic context I equate mock intrigue with the more comic, often blackly comic and absurdist, satirical aspects of the narrator—his life, his perceptions, and, behind him, Welch's perceptions. Mock intrigue is also extended to those people, ideas, and events that affect the narrator and are affected by him—experiences never truly assimilated by him, never puzzled out—or if they are understood, they are taken as nothing much more than trifles.

Seen this way, the scheme of the book is such that the dominant "mystery" includes the death of the narrator's brother, Mose; the death of the narrator's father, First Raise; the true identity of Yellow Calf and his relationship with the narrator's grandmother, and the larger genealogy of the Blackfeet peoples; the true nature of the narrator's injury—just how he came to suffer from his "wounded knee" and what caused his initial and ostensibly terminally benumbed, winterized mental and emotional state. Certainly the separate "mysteries" of all these major facets of the novel are intricately interrelated once they are "figured out" by the narrator and dramatized and explained for the reader who is working just as hard as the narrator throughout the book—but by means of ratiocination and inference more than memory (although that is also a factor)—to find out just what is happening in the narrator's present and what went on in his past. Past and present converge variously throughout the novel, but more powerfully after the narrator's grandmother dies and he is once again digging a grave. At that point the narrator's repressed trauma over the death of Mose (and, by extension, of First Raise) is not only understood but felt—with all the collision force of the ill-fated, careening automobile striking Mose and his horse, as if in some kind of "explosive" movie of the mind. Architectonically this is accomplished by means of Welch's skillful use of suspense, of foreshadowing and flashbacks, of expanding and reflexive imagery and symbolism.

In comparison to the actual experience of reading the novel, of figuring things out, attempting methodically to explain Welch's use of suspenseful and dynamic imagery is a paltry enterprise. The novel is so tightly and subtly stitched, so supremely coherent and unified in spite of the ultimately superficial, always deceptive confusion, that an explanation of one element under the heading of "mystery" soon leads to another subheading and eventually to another major heading of "mock intrigue." This is a reminder that a consideration of mystery, as I have outlined its association with the tragic aspects of the book, soon turns to a consideration of mock intrigue.

The idea of the narrator's "wounded knee," as a symbol or objective correlative of both his physical and psychic injury sustained when he is thrown from Bird (that great white horse) at the scene of his brother's death on a wintry Montana highway, is one such instance of Welch's skill in merging mystery and mock intrigue. The narrator's numb but aching knee is not just a knee but also a tragicomic implied pun, a joke, played on both the narrator and the audience, on both the processes of history and fiction. There are many such merged, ironic instances, joinings of mystery and mock intrigue (often they are instances of dramatic irony), where Welch allows the reader significant clues that add another whole dimension of detective role-playing by the reader, beyond fiction and into the even more baffling sequence of cause and effect called history.

The entire interpolated, seemingly digressive history of Yellow Calf and grandmother and the winter he spent looking after her when she was abandoned by the Blackfeet tribe and his own revealed identity as a Blackfeet rather than a Gros Ventre is another episode suggestive of the tragic mysteries and comic intrigues of both fiction and history, invented and real, experienced and told. Another example of how Welch merges mystery with mock intrigue is his treatment of the narrator's Cree girl-friend, her role as antagonist to grandmother, her absconding with the narrator's ironically personal but valueless possessions of razor and gun, and her escape, which provides the overall framework for the journey (actually several journeys) the narrator must take to find her. As a runaway, pictured at one point with green, creme-de-menthe coated teeth, at once the potential object of the narrator's love and of grandmother's hate and plotted assassination, Agnes is a comprehensive vehicle for Welch's nicely confused (confused but controlled) portrayal of a simultaneously meaningless and meaningful love.

If the search for Agnes provides the framework for the characters and events that contribute to the mock intrigue of the novel, the narrator's relationships with other characters give the novel's mock intrigue its substance. Good natured and self-serving Lame Bull and moaning Teresa; Ferdinand Horn and his bespectacled, inquiring wife; flashy cowboy Ray Long Knife and Belva, his hungry mother; Teresa and her clandestine relationship with Father Kitteredge, the priest in Harlem, as well as her relationship with her sons, Mose and the narrator, her first husband, First Raise, and with her reputed father, the half-breed drifter, Doagie—all of these intrigues, which take as their locale Earthboy ranch, provide one important nodality.

The highway between the towns, with their endless string of bars, and the towns themselves provide two other nodalities that give substance to the mock intrigue in the novel. The women the narrator meets on the road to his discoveries and rememberings as he sallies forth, a pathetic, drunken, and debilitated picaro, up and down the valley from the Earthboy ranch and his reservation home—from Dodson to Malta to Harlem to Havre and back again—provide even more substance to his "quest" for Agnes. These women include the bosomy barmaid in Malta; the tattooed mother, Malvina, in Harlem; and the wanton Marlene in Havre. Laced throughout the narrator's search for Agnes; his pursuit by her brother, Dougie (easily and significantly confused by the reader with Teresa's alleged father and the narrator's reputed grandfather, Doagie); and the narrator's promiscuous sexual escapades is his utterly confusing and anticlimactic involvement with the fugitive from New York, the "airplane man" whose grand plan for getaway across the border into Canada, in, of all things, a Ford Falcon, instigates some of the most hilarious and nonsensical scenes in the novel.

It is admittedly dangerous to reduce a novel as complex as *Winter in the Blood* to the two categories of mystery on the one hand and mock intrigue on the other—with a buffer zone of sorts resting in between where the two elements overlap. For present purposes, analysis is limited to the characters of Mose and the "airplane man" and their respective contributions to the mystery and mock intrigue, the tragedy and the comedy of the book.

The reader does not discover what really happened to Mose, does not find out the details of his death, until the end of Part Three, 163 pages into the 199-page novel. The reader is aware from the beginning of the novel that Mose is dead and so is his father, First Raise. The reader has clues concerning the way in which Mose died; but for all practical purposes Mose's death is a mystery. And because the narrator has repressed the anguish of his brother's death, the "mystery" of it extends to the narrator. Through Welch's manipulations, the book builds on its most tragic level to the dramatic reenactment of that death—so that both the narrator and the reader actually "see" the accident again (in the case of the narrator), and for the first time (in the case of the reader):

> I couldn't have seen it—we were still moving in the
> opposite direction, the tears, the dark and wind in my
> eyes—the movie exploded whitely in my brain, and
> I saw the futile lurch of the car as the brake lights
> popped, the horse's shoulder caving before the fender,
> the horse spinning so that its rear end smashed into the
> door, the smaller figure flying slowly over the top of
> the car to land with the hush of a stuffed doll.
> The calf stopped at the sound of collision. Bird
> jolted down the slope of the shoulder and I tumbled
> from his back, down into the dark weeds. I felt my
> knee strike something hard, a rock maybe, or a culvert,
> then the numbness. (p. 163)

For the narrator, this reenactment, this dredged-up recollection is a psychological and emotional catharsis that seems to amount to a degree of improvement, ironically, in his zombielike condition, a thawing out of his metaphorical "winterized" sense of death. The physical death had been Mose's, but the complementary "spirited" drunken driver collided with Mose and his horse. At the same moment in the novel, the cause of the narrator's injured knee and its literal and figurative significance also becomes clear. He too had suffered a collision, with either a rock or a culvert, when he sailed off of Bird (paralleling Mose's flight) and smashed his leg. But not everything is known even yet. Mysteries still remain. Who was the driver? Was his bad breath caused by alcohol? What did the narrator's knee hit, exactly? Even upon this final revelation, questions linger behind the answers. Inference suffices rather than certainty.

Images of explosion and collision cluster around the revelation of the circumstances of Mose's death, and serve by way of widening referents to supplement the solution of the mystery of why the narrator is so disoriented, so dazed, so punchy. All of the fists in the face and all of the collision and car imagery—Lame Bull punching Raymond Long Knife; Dougie slugging the narrator, who hitches a ride back home from Havre; the "black pickup" that roars past him with Teresa and Lame Bull inside; the dark-green Hudson of Ferdinand and Mrs. Horn—build up to and recede from the moment and the memory of Mose's death. Similarly, the pervasive imagery of winter, of literal and figurative coldness, and the persistent animal imagery reinforce the cause-and-effect mystery behind Mose's death. But all the imagery that creates and unravels the mysteries surrounding Mose's death only serves to underscore the biggest mystery of all: "Why did Mose have to die?" "Why Mose?" "Why death?" Welch, the narrator, and the reader are all left with that imponderable, dramatized yet again at the graveside of grandmother—and in the final whinnying of the other horses for Bird.

For the narrator, First Raise's death is only superficially more understandable than Mose's death. And as with Mose's death, it is not clear at the beginning of the novel that the death of First Raise—found frozen in a borrow pit across from the Earthboy place—is an imagistic repetition of the cold weather when the narrator and Mose drove First Raise's cattle across that fateful highway. And it is not at all clear at the start that First Raise's death is directly linked to the death of Mose. Grandmother's grave, Mose's grave, First Raise's grave are all part of the same mystery. Significantly, the narrator remembers Mose's death, as fully as he is capable, in the family cemetery plot. It is not initially obvious that First Raise's death was caused as much by guilt and grief as it was by drink and exposure. We learn that it is First Raise who makes the request for the cattle drive, arranges it and sends the boys off, ironically, with love and a good breakfast—as the pathos of the story would have it. It is First Raise who primes that particular mystery.

Teresa insists that it was an anonymous "they" who found First Raise alongside the road. The narrator remembers riding the highway, looking in the borrow pits, and thinks that "we," that the family and not "they," found First Raise's frozen body. And as the confusion about so many things multiplies (including the mystery and the mock intrigue of whether First Raise or Teresa or somebody else killed Amos), the narrator's unreliability grows. Moreover, this unreliability is in itself mysterious.

In addition to being connected to the tragic mystery of Mose's death, First Raise is connected to the mystery of the narrator's ancestry and identity. It is First Raise who takes the narrator, when still a child, to visit Yellow Calf one winter. This detail is remembered only after the narrator's realization that Yellow Calf is his grandfather; that he is Teresa's father—not the half-white drifter, Doagie. (The confusion of Doagie's name with Dougie; of Raymond Long Knife's name with the soldiers dubbed the Long Knives; of Marlene with Malvina; of Yellow Calf with his outrageous nickname of Batman; of the New Yorker's alias, "airplane man"—all of the multiple and duplicate names serve likewise to heighten the confusion.)

As a kind of mock-epic, senile, "blind seer," Yellow Calf knows the answers to many mysteries—those of ancestry learned through his own experiences as a hunter and provider for grandmother during that one particularly hard, historic, loving winter—and he knows those answers learned from the deer and his own internalized, visionary secrets. During his visits with Yellow Calf the narrator must tease out some of the answers to those mysteries. Yellow Calf is assuredly an instance of mock intrigue and comedy. But the mysteries to which he knows the answers, and which First Raise realized much before the narrator does, play heavily on the narrator's own alienation and his mystery of identity. Until such mysteries are answered, the faces of First Raise, of the drifter, Doagie, of Yellow Calf, of the New York fugitive, and even of the narrator himself, including his disputed age, will remain confused.

That confusion is reinforced by the vitally ancient ages of Bird and the spinster cow. The deliberate ambiguities of whether or not the spinster cow the narrator attempts to save at the end of the novel is indeed the same animal that balked at the time of Mose's accident, and of Bird's age and implied death, also heighten the mysteries of just who the narrator was and who he is now.

The biggest comic mock intrigue surrounds the identity and motivation of the man from New York, the "airplane man," who is on the lam and in Montana presumably to make a getaway across the border into Canada. The narrator's initial and recurrent meetings with the New York fugitive provide a major focus for the element of mock intrigue. The airplane man is even more anonymous than the narrator and although less tragically mysterious, he is nevertheless just as comically intriguing.

Their first meeting comes in Malta, in the ironic squalor of the Pomp Room. That meeting begins on a ludicrous note of irony and ambiguity which establishes the terms for all their future dealings. The airplane man, although running away from his past life, attempts to prove to the narrator that he is indeed from New York—and shows him his credit card to "prove" it. He is dressed in khaki and reminds the narrator, significantly, of the lion hunters (known intimately not from life but from the printed page as McLeod and Henderson) whom he has read about in the *Sports Afield* story which works as an interpolated tale in the opening pages of the novel and as an expansive image throughout. That hunt went around in circles—and so does the narrator's "hunt" for the airplane man's identity and past as the narrator circles his way between towns and the ranch looking for Agnes and his possessions. First Raise's perpetually planned hunt in Glacier National Park is another echo of similar futility.

The airplane man announces that he was at one time a rich man, and that he had a wife and two daughters. But his purpose is to solve the problems that the narrator does not remember having. Despite his avowal to help the narrator solve his problems, the New Yorker continues to talk about his own life—continues to offer clues as to who he is and why he is in Montana and at the moment talking to someone he doesn't even know. For a presumed fugitive he is strangely talkative. He garrulously tells the narrator that he was on his way to the Middle East, ready to board a plane, when he tore up his tickets in front of "her," picked up his fishing gear, and drove away. Who "she" is, the narrator and the reader can only guess—for the airplane man assumes, again ironically, thanks to Welch, that the narrator and the reader know more than we do. Each spoken and implied detail leads circuitously to add to the mock intrigue, the humor of the situation as event and dialog.

After an argument about catching fish where none are to be caught, the argument becomes even more bizarre with confusions about Minnesota and the promise of the best steak in—of all the crazy places—Kalamazoo, if they don't catch any fish. There is more than one kind of fishing expedition going on here. And the hunting and fishing imagery all reinforce the intrigue. The reader, and even the narrator, soon realize that there is an absurdity present that goes beyond the burblings of two ordinary drunks.

To heighten the zaniness of the intrigue, two men dressed in suits that smell of wet wool come into the bar (more like rain-drenched sheepherders than special agents). They move "down the bar like cows on slick ice" (p. 57), an inherently comic image but one that also conjures up the scene of Mose's death. The bartender "stalks" them down the other side of the bar on a miniature "tailing" mission of his own. The two men are ostensibly followed by the airplane man. Confusion increases when a fish called "gold eyes" is introduced into the conversation and the two men in suits are turned to as referees in the dispute (the unlikeliest of roles), while the barmaid blows smoke rings to obfuscate things visually with the smoke and its symbolic circles—from a cigarette, a source, ironically undiscovered by the narrator.

As pursued and pursuers disagree about whether or not local fishing waters are clear or muddy (another symbolic obfuscation), the discussion continues in its own way of comic misunderstandings. And when the airplane man thinks that he recognizes the barmaid from times either in Bismarck, Minneapolis, Chicago, Seattle, or San Francisco—from one end of the country to the other—the inane befuddlement compounds itself in a string of totally "off the wall" non sequiturs about roses and morning glories and cats and birthmarks. While the airplane man tries to pin down his identification, not of himself this time, but of the barmaid, she attempts to explain to the narrator why she is only partially recognizable to the airplane man:

> "He used to pay me. That's why I hated it. He used to pay me a dollar to dance for him." She laughed. "It was such fun, twirling around the room, faster and faster until I must have been a blur. That's why he forgets my face." (p. 59)

What did she hate? She says, contradictorily, that she thought the dancing fun—but, again, ironically, and somewhat pathetically, because she became a blur: like countless others in the novel. The full-blown mock intrigue of the scene is apparent especially at the end when the New Yorker makes his exit while the narrator and the barmaid talk:

> The airplane man glared at her. Suddenly he jerked upright and roared [like the lion in the *Sports Afield* story?]—I thought first suit had stuck a knife in his back—then rushed her, arms extended as if to hug or strangle her. At the last instant, he swerved and hit the door, plunging into the night. (p. 61)

The obfuscation of the smoke in the barroom has become more ominously and mysteriously the night itself. By utilizing the vocabulary and incident of murder mystery and spy thriller, Welch, on the level of parody, is having great fun. But there is also the hint, created by the ambiguous and ironic hopelessness the characters face, that the mystery and oblivion of the night will, in keeping with the strain of naturalism in the novel, engulf them all.

Thus, the barmaid from Malta is lost in as much darkness of anonymity as is the New Yorker, and the narrator, and the two men in suits; and so is the old man, who in a later scene is identified as a spy by the airplane man (one of a cadre of comic types in his pursuit), and who, after that identification, falls face first into his bowl of oatmeal. Here, Welch's range of mock intrigue dramatizes the sad hilarity of life as a bad joke.

On several levels, then, the network of escapes and pursuits expands into a mass of comic tangles: the narrator pursues Agnes and at the same time flees from her brother and the redheaded cowboy whom the narrator helps Doagie roll; the New Yorker flees from his high living past, pursued by the paranoia of real and imagined spies and FBI agents, and tries to make the narrator the instrument of his extravagant escape; grandmother, thinking of a paring knife, plots the assassination of Agnes as if she merits the stature of a long-standing Cree enemy. The "stacked" barmaid from Malta; Malvina, the woman in Harlem with the intriguing initials, "J.R.," tattooed on her hand, and the mother of an inscrutable, sinister son about as comically threatening as the oatmeal man; Marlene, the rotten-toothed floozy who literally picks up the narrator from the sidewalks of Havre (echoing First Raise's position in the barrow pit)—all of these characters are introduced by Welch as laminations of the element of mock intrigue, but tend ultimately to merge always, and reciprocally, with the more tragic mysteries of the book.

Like all fine novels and like Welch's subsequent novels, *Winter in the Blood* invites new insights, new connections each time it is read. There are countless scenes, numerous elements that hold up again and again, analysis after analysis (both because of and in spite of analysis). When the book is read as a tragicomedy about the confusions of life amplified through literature, it is possible to classify a main structural and thematic element in the novel as the interplay of mystery and mock intrigue.

And behind the humor and the pathos at each juncture in the Montana and mind journey of an anonymous American Indian narrator is the author, James Welch, who, although he knows the answers to the tragic mysteries and comic intrigues of his own novelistic creation, succeeds in communicating to the reader a modernist, at once realistic and surrealistic, version of what Keats mysteriously termed, when looking not at Montana but at the Elgin Marbles, a "shadow of a magnitude."

THE DEATH OF JIM LONEY

Welch's second novel, *The Death of Jim Loney*, portrays, perhaps better than any other contemporary Native American novel, the sad and melancholy, if not tragic results of the inversions, transmutations, and corruptions of indigenous hunting motives, of rights gone wrong and of self-willed alienation unto death. The motif is first hinted at in *Winter in the Blood*. But in *The Death of Jim Loney* Welch gives it much greater form. Jim Loney, a drunken, has-been high-school basketball star, accompanies his old high-school buddy, Myron Pretty Weasel, on a fateful hunting trip near Harlem, their Montana home along the Milk River. It is a deer hunt, or ostensibly so, but it is a hunt of a different order than other hunts in American Indian literature. It ends tragically, in the murder of a human rather than an animal, in the hunter becoming the hunted. But the indigenous, atavistic hunting glories that provide a baseline or subtext for a majority of hunts and hunters in the Native American novel exist in *Loney* in a much more distant, confused mythic past.

Loney, potentially even more heroic as a hunter than he was as a high-school basketball hero, either deliberately or accidentally (he himself is confused), shoots his friend, either thinking that Pretty Weasel was or knowing that he wasn't a bear charging out of the cattails by the slough at McFarland's place—a dark shape charging out of his and Pretty Weasel's high-school years, out of their boyhood pheasant hunts, out of the more distant aboriginal and mythic past. The killing of Pretty Weasel becomes the motive for the lonely resolve which initiates not just the manhunt for Loney, but Loney's hunt for his own best death, symbolized throughout by an imagistic dark bird, associated, at least in part, with both the predatory and soaring qualities of an eagle.

Portrayed imagistically in his death (a kind of suicidal sacrifice to the gods of the hunt) as both the counterpart of the bear he thought was Pretty Weasel when he killed him, and as a bird that metaphorically has been haunting and hunting his dreams, Loney's own physical offering of his body to the high-powered, scope-mounted "hunting" rifle of the Indian policeman, Quentin Doore, is finally of no consequence to him. Nor is it of consequence, really, to his upscale sister, Kate, nor to his Texas schoolteacher girlfriend, Rhea's sexual curiosities and yearnings, nor definitely to his father's spiteful accusations and revelations. It is the freeing of his spirit, of his "dark bird," which matters. It is a freeing and a longing for transcendence which parallels N. Scott Momaday's great descriptions in *House Made of Dawn*, his designs in having Abel kill the once glorious and free female eagle held, again darkly, in captivity.

Welch's description of Loney's murder/suicide, which takes place, significantly, in the Bearpaw mountains, is similarly motivated by an acknowledgment by Loney that hunters of the right sort are owed the right of freedom and release, even, paradoxically, the freedom of their prey. Here is Welch's account of Loney's death—the death of a bird, an "eagle" of another, human sort:

That is what you wanted, he thought, and that was the
last thought left to him. He stood and he felt a dimness
in his head and he took two steps and he felt something
sharp in his stomach as though someone had jabbed
him with a stick. And he fell, and as he was falling he
felt a harsh wind where there was none and the last
thing he saw were the beating wings of a dark bird as
it climbed to a distant place.[3]

Just as Momaday uses much bird and animal imagery to reinforce the
dominance of the eagle(s) and the bear, so too does Welch construct such
a bestiary. The imagery of the dark, transcendent, haunting/hunting
bird—an analog to Loney himself—is especially underscored by descriptions of pheasants and the pheasant hunts he and Pretty Weasel went on
as boys.

One on the fly [Loney remembered] and two on the
ground. Two on the fly. Once all three on the fly.
Loney remembered his frustration as he squeezed off
his single shot at a running cock, then the whir of his
wings as Loney struggled to reload. Once he even carried his shells in him mouth so he wouldn't have to dig
in a pocket, but his tongue turned gray and he thought
he had lead poisoning. (pp. 95–96)

Like the pheasants he attempts to shoot, like Pretty Weasel, bearlike in
his dark size and mass, Loney, indeed, does get lead poisoning of the most
deadly variety.

When he shoots Pretty Weasel, Loney is trying to remember the coded
whistle they had used as kids hunting pheasants and rabbits. There was
"a quick *wheet*, then a pause, and in that pause, he forgot the rest of it. . . .
Then he heard the brittle crashing of the dry stalks and he saw the darkness of it, its immense darkness in that dazzling day, and he thrust the gun
to his cheek and he felt the recoil and he saw the astonished look on
Pretty Weasel's face as he stumbled two steps back and sat down in the
crackling cattails" (pp. 119–20).

The vague "it," as it crashes toward Loney and his reflexive response,
might be viewed as a kind of objective correlative for the twisted and
knotted assurances and denials, guarantees and betrayals that cluster
around and give some kind of lingering presence to indigenous "rights,"
just as Loney's attempted whistle, though belated, gives notice and alarm
and recognition to Pretty Weasel as man-animal. Native American liter-

ature, enhanced by Welch's work, affords much concern with and insight into the ways and means of the law, particularly as it has given both shape and distortion to aboriginal and indigenous rights in judging the Indian hunter, more times than not, as a criminal rather than a hero.

Given the more or less stock plot of tragedy, the title of Welch's novel, and the first couple of pages (even the Malcolm Lowry epigraph), there's little doubt about Jim Loney's antiheroic albeit tragic destiny. He will die. He wants to die. Alone. It's purely a matter of how—and of why. It's not that people—including Pretty Weasel—don't care for him. There's an ancillary plot and a host of characters beyond Myron Pretty Weasel.

Loney's older sister, Kate, a beautifully chic, liberated, successful woman who lives in Washington, D.C., and lectures on "education" all over the country, surely loves Jim Loney in loyal, blood-kin ways, and possibly in slightly sexual, slightly incestuous ways—or so it is suggested. Once a replacement mother to Jim, Kate returns to Montana to rescue her brother from self-destruction. But Kate can't stay in Montana, and Jim must stay out of a will to die.

Kate's competitor in attempted salvation is Rhea Davis, a Texas belle winding up a schoolteaching stint in the hinterlands of Big Sky country. Rhea, given her background of Anglo wealth and privilege down South, is surprised (as is Jim, who can't believe his own worth) that her fling with someone society might view as a drunken, despondent Indian has turned to real love. And in spite of the possibility that she can lure Loney away to a new, purposeful life in Seattle, Loney is compelled to explore loneliness and the willful dramatization, the directing and staging of Pretty Weasel's death and Loney's own compounding death wish.

This "tragedy of blood" involves not just the demise of a onetime high-school friend and basketball teammate, but Loney's rejection of such lovely would-be deliverers as Kate and Rhea, and the loss of even more fundamental friends like his old dog, Swipsey, found frozen to death in street mud one morning; the longtime companionship of momentary mourner and buddy Amos After Buffalo, a symbolic boy (representative perhaps of Loney's own childhood hopes and dreams, as well as those of Indian people); the evaporation of fond yet vague memories of Sandra, his childhood guardian and the only woman Loney ever truly loved; and—the climactic event that precipitates Loney's final destruction wherein the hunter becomes the hunted—the shooting (call it murder?) of Myron Pretty Weasel.

And in keeping with the ironic, tragic turn of things, Loney's rambling father, Ike (a father in name only), plays a crucial role in his son's script and leads the vengeful Indian policeman, Doore, and the more compassionate Painter Barthelme to the selected sacrificial spot in Mission Canyon.

The powerful ending to a poignantly rendered descent into the maelstrom, into death, echoes the temper of the world of modernist angst and misadventure traversed by Malcolm Lowry in *Under the Volcano*, the work Welch quotes by way of epigraph. Thus, if little cheerfulness or celebration (though plenty of black humor) exists in *The Death of Jim Loney*, it may be well to recall the paradox that it lies within the cathartic power of tragic literature—in this instance, of Jim Welch writing about the deaths of two friends; about the death of Loney himself, who may be viewed (at least in part) as Welch's fictional doppelgänger—to affirm life, ours as well as that of the modern American, Native American novel.

FOOLS CROW

To read the novels of James Welch is to realize that contemporary Native American literature is puzzlingly redundant, a redundancy more significant than recurring stock scenes and characters may at first suggest. Echoes of D'Arcy McNickle's *The Surrounded* (1936) are heard in N. Scott Momaday's *House Made of Dawn*; and shades of these two tellings are found in more recent Indian fictions like Leslie Silko's *Ceremony* (1977) and Welch's *Winter in the Blood* and *The Death of Jim Loney*. Along with John G. Neihardt's rendering of Black Elk's autobiography, *Black Elk Speaks* (1932) and other Native American oral and written tellings, McNickle's and Momaday's works seem more prototypical, more authentic, with each passing year.

It is, moreover, the poetry of "singers" like Ray Anthony Young Bear, Simon J. Ortiz, Joy Harjo, Wendy Rose, the late William Oandasan, Geary Hobson, Linda Hogan, and, again, Welch—especially in *Riding the Earthboy Forty* (1971; rev. ed., 1975)—that brings into greater focus the reason for this noticeable recurrence of seemingly antiheroic, alienated, and benumbed protagonists, singers, and speakers at odds with their pasts and the times and places in which they find themselves. It is the simultaneous impetus of atavism and modernism—the need, as Young Bear phrases it, "to be there, standing beside our grandfathers, being ourselves" and by meeting that need, to bring meaning to the twentieth-century predicament.

Winter in the Blood and *The Death of Jim Loney* are decidedly modern in their stories and settings—and yet in both works Welch strives to work backward into history, into the times and tellings of older generations, older ways of knowing and perceiving. He does this, characteristically, by juxtaposing stories of the present with stories of the past, the stories (histories, biographies, myths, and dreams) of an individual—a central protagonist and center of consciousness—with the larger stories and histories of that protagonist's friends, family, and culture, all augmented and given texture by glimpses of the life stories of non-Native Americans who pass through the lives of Welch's protagonists.

In *Fools Crow*, Welch reaches back even further into the past and arrives more fully than ever at that backward-looking destination that so preoccupies him; arrives both as a Blackfeet/Gros Ventre inheritor and keeper of his heritage and as an artist. In his book he stands from beginning to end beside his grandfathers and grandmothers—and he takes the reader with him back to those times when the Montana Blackfeet enjoyed just being themselves.

Insofar as the historical novel as genre allows for this kind of time travel, *Fools Crow* is a masterwork of linguistic and narrative transporting. An affirmation of the power of the word—the word as medicine, as is so often the theme in contemporary Native American literature—it also affirms the necessity for an individual, a family, and a culture not only to rely on but to identify itself, know its very dreaming, becoming, and ending *in and through* storytelling and myth. But it is not just the conventions of the historical novel that allow Welch to both dramatize and, in effect, advocate this necessity.

Welch makes story every bit as important as history by structuring his novel around several levels of storytelling and portraying several storytellers. Thus Welch attempts to tell his larger story, his novel, in many voices, in many modes—relying especially on the surrealism of dreams, the narrative and cultural assumptions of myth, and the stylistic potential of something approximating the techniques of magic realism. As a result, storytelling becomes not just the means and process of *Fools Crow*; rather, it becomes the very subject itself.

Because of these layers, this texturing, *Fools Crow* is an ambitious novel, one that dares to try many things and thus dares to risk large failures—especially the potential failure of fragmentation and disunity. In spite of its tendency toward digression and what some might regard as a lack of tightness and coherence, *Fools Crow* succeeds precisely because of its ambition and its daring, its multilevel narrative juxtapositions and interpolations.

For in this manner, Welch not only confirms the traditions of the novel—reaching all the way back to Cervantes and Fielding and other earlier counterparts with their layering of stories within stories within stories—he confirms (through his various narrations and dramatizations) the oral impulse of narrative, especially of Native American cultures, and he confirms the potential and resiliency of the novel, both the life of the novel and why it matters, as D. H. Lawrence insisted, as the one bright book of life.

Fools Crow has an epic sweep in that it offers an account of gods working their ways on humankind trying to influence the will of the gods, of nature, and of destiny. Welch tells the story of a small but noble band of Pikunis Indians (that is, Blackfeet) known as the Lone Eaters facing the death of their gods and their culture at the hands of the U.S. government and its "seizers," more gloriously and ethnocentrically known as the United States Cavalry.

One of Welch's techniques in re-creating the world of the Lone Eaters is linguistic. He invents his own scheme of naming which, whether real or an approximation, has the intended effect of establishing an older (but for the reader newer) way of knowing.

The other two tribes of the Blackfeet are known as Kainahs and Siksikas. Important characters in the events portrayed are White Man's Dog (become Fools Crow); his father, Rides-at-the-door; his friends Fast Horse and Yellow Kidney; Fast Horse's father and keeper of the Beaver Medicine, Boss Ribs; Yellow Kidney's wife, Heavy Shield Woman, and her daughter, Red Paint, whom White Man's Dog marries; the renegade Owl Child and his band, who soon enlist Fast Horse in their marauding raids on whites; and White Man's Dog's mentor—the many-faces man, the shaman Mik-api. Whites are the Napikwans. Winter is known here as Cold Maker; the moon is Night Red Light; horses are known as blackhorn runners, while buffalo are called the blackhorns. White Man's Dog's power animal, the wolverine, is skunk bear. Woodbiter is the beaver. And so it goes, at once magical and real.

Such naming can be frivolous, notably when these presumably archaic labels butt up against more contemporary vocabulary. (Ruth Beebe Hill's *Hanta Yo* [1979] is probably the silliest attempt at creating allegedly authentic idiomatic phrases and glossary.) But such "silliness" is Welch's gamble, a risk he must take in order to transport the reader back as far as the novel, written within its conventions and in English, will allow and still re-create an older and other language and culture and worldview. There is, of course, not only much of magic realism in all this, but something of fable and fantasy as well.

The historical event—if it can be called that—to which *Fools Crow* builds, assuming the ethnocentrism and "knowing" of Anglo-American historiography, is the Marias River massacre in the winter of 1870 when 173 Blackfeet, mostly women and children in the band of Chief Heavy Runner, were slaughtered in an attempt to halt the raiding of white settlers by a small group of renegades (that is, the band of Owl Child and Fast Horse in terms of the novel).

The historical period of *Fools Crow* is the three years from 1867 to 1870 and a bit beyond. Welch not only knows this event through the stories of his people—most particularly his father and grandmother—but he also read five or so books on the "history" of that time, including *My Life as an Indian* by J. W. Schultz (1907).[4] Welch says this about the interaction of story and history as they converge in *Fools Crow*:

> Even though Schultz's period was a little after mine he still gives us a feeling for what the people were like, so I read him and I read about four other books. My Dad's grandmother had lived with him and survived that massacre on the Marias. She told him about that and several other things about the Blackfeet's lives before the whites. And he told me all these stories. At first that was my main idea, to just go by what my father had told me, but then I realized what I had to do, I had to set the novel in a period of history, I had to be faintly accurate.[5]

The winter of January 1870 was a terrible one for the Blackfeet, who were suffering from an especially severe epidemic of smallpox that killed scores of people. After the massacre and smallpox the Blackfeet were never a military menace to the U.S. Cavalry again-nor much of a "problem" to white settlers.

In *Winter in the Blood*, Welch, mainly through the interpolated revelations of the old, blind seer Yellow Calf, and the guesses and conclusions of the nameless narrator, Yellow Calf's grandson, tells of the harsh times his turn-of-the-century ancestors experienced in warding off hunger, disease, and the encroaching white civilization. In *Fools Crow* Welch paints a panoramic picture of the events outlined in Yellow Calf's life history—how the Anglo-American conceptions of progress, the future, Manifest Destiny, and "History," aided by treaties, whiskey, and smallpox, and the like, all but put an end to the Blackfeet and other Plains Indians.

One of the many intriguing interpolated stories in *Fools Crow* (albeit a minor one), in this case a continuing story picked up allusively from *Winter in the Blood*, is the account of the birth of Yellow Calf, presumably the old "Bat-Man" character of the same name in the latter novel.

It is Yellow Kidney who wanted to live to see his grandson named Yellow Calf, for he had seen, on his last quest, a buffalo cow and her yellow calf grazing on a hillside. Yellow Kidney considers the buffalo calf a gift from the Sun Chief and an emblem of forgiveness for his sleeping with a Crow woman infected, unbeknownst to him, with smallpox—an event that takes place early in the novel and provides the motivation for not only Yellow Kidney's story, his demise and death, but for his final act of courage and cleansing, and for White Man's Dog's honorable protection of Yellow Kidney's wife and daughter.

Thus Welch weaves the later story of old Yellow Calf in *Winter in the Blood* with the earlier story of his grandfather, Yellow Kidney, and his epiphany which serves as a naming and an incipient life-telling. When the young yellow buffalo calf looks up at Yellow Kidney he cannot kill it: "Instead, he would take his name for his grandson. Yellow Calf. A strong name, one that would someday be spoken with fear in the camps of the enemies."[6] The allusiveness is not exact, for Yellow Kidney does not live to see and name his grandson; and Yellow Calf himself seems to live in the world of *Winter in the Blood* contemporaneously with his grandfather. But it is indicative of Welch's striving to tell and tell again the stories of the genealogy of the Blackfeet, the lives of his own ancestors—to be there with them again.

In *Fools Crow*, White Man's Dog provides the center of consciousness from which the coming of the end is told. His story of apocalypse is all the more tragic because, thanks to Welch's artistry, it is also a grand and mythic story of initiation and maturation, of dream and prophecy told and lived. White Man's Dog does not have the luxury of telling these events in retrospect from the perspective of his old age. The endings to the various stories come at the zenith of his life, converging with his adulthood, his marriage and fatherhood, and his heroic rebirth as Fools Crow, a warrior destined to lead his people in their final days.

His ability to fool his Crow enemies and his refusal to fool himself or his people about their coming doom are foretold in his visionary transcendence into the surreal "Backbone of the world," home of Feather Woman, a prime mythic cause for the Pikunis' misfortune. His brave deeds as a raider of Crow horses; his steadfastness in standing beside the braggart Fast Horse in his ostracism; his friendship with Yellow Kidney and providing for his family (as Yellow Calf had for old Grandma in *Winter in the Blood*); his "apprenticeship" with Mik-api, and his resultant alliance with Raven and the successful salvation of Skunk Bear from the killing traps of the Nipikwan—in all of these ways and throughout their tellings, White Man's Dog become Fools Crow proves equal to the potential power and *efficacy* of the word.

Although he is aided in his quest for name and honor by Mik-api, the many-faces man, and by raven and wolverine, Fools Crow is unable to save either his people or himself. But his story, and behind that, Welch's novel, holds forth at least a promise of the triumph of the human spirit. Fools Crow's story suggests allegorical interpretations of not just the survival of the Blackfeet at the dawn of the twentieth century, but of the problematic survival of humanity, and even the biosphere.

To achieve this effect, this new beginning out of a past ending, Welch takes the reader through a complicated network of subplots, substories, and characters as he creates a psychological and linguistic facsimile of Blackfeet culture. Alternating between realism and surrealism, states of consciousness and subconsciousness, dreamscape reality and everyday waking reality, Welch makes the tried and true, now conventional techniques of stream-of-consciousness narration seem rather antiquated if not naive. Such chance taking soon overcomes conservative longings for symmetry and tidiness. All in all, the truths of fiction win out and underscore the mysteries of history, the magic of story. Fools Crow the character and *Fools Crow* the novel confirm that Native American literature, both contemporary novel and poetry, establishes like no other literature being written today the ineffable link between primitivism and modernism.

Human history, as Freud and Norman O. Brown, among others, suggest, may be an eternal struggle between life and death, now and again tilting and plunging further toward utter obliteration. But if there is an ultimate argument to be made in favor of life and its telling, a work like *Fools Crow* helps right the balance.

The Indian Lawyer

Contemporary Native American fiction obviously has, almost by its very nature, strong historical and political commitments. History almost defines the genre, provoking many intriguing questions about the old issues of reality and illusion, fact and fiction, politics and art. Welch's fiction invites such considerations.

Like other minority American writers since the 1960s, recent Native American fictionists have combined history and story, art and advocacy to advance not just the cause of the novel and the short story—as all authors of merit, regardless of race or ethnicity, implicitly seek to do—but to advance the cause of the downtrodden, the outsider, the misfit, the loser—to make a case for "otherness."

Especially since midcentury (but in accord with much older assumptions and attitudes) Native American novelists have demonstrated and implicitly argued for (through dramatizations and dialogue) the relativity of otherness. They have argued against the traditional ethnocentric, reductive Euro-American characterizations of American Indians and white/ Indian encounters as if they were, historically, part of some presumed, single "American" experience centered totally on non-Indian causality, namely Eurocentric initiations, reactions, interpretations, and justifications.

The New History and New Literary History of the 1980s and 1990s, particularly in relation to the American West, have transvaluated many of the manly motives, many of the "American" triumphs of the Old West into embarrassments and failures so that much of the "winning" of the Old West is now viewed as predicated on racism, sexism, cruelty, and violence. Ironically, losers in Native American fiction are often winners in the "losing," especially in willfully rejecting Americanization rather than passively accepting defeat. Such ironic transvaluations provide a different perspective of history and of advocacy.

William Carlos Williams's *In the American Grain* (1925) serves as an illustrious example of how history, advocacy, and art combined early in this century, through the author's idiosyncratic selection of texts and revisionist retellings of old narratives that promulgated the predominantly WASP, male, New England literary canon. His villain was not the Indian, but the Puritan. His heroes and heroines were darker skinned, Native American, indigenous to the continent or natural American icons like Daniel Boone. Williams's subversions of the American traditions perhaps more effectively reversed Euro-American exoticism than did any other modern American author.

Welch, among contemporary Native American novelists, especially in *The Indian Lawyer* (1990), extends and deepens the American grain as Williams presented it. Through Welch's characterization of Sylvester Yellow Calf, the Blackfeet attorney of the novel's title, as a "new Warrior," through the thematic use of new cultural and racial assumptions and relationships in a new West, and through Yellow Calf's political agenda in his aborted candidacy for Congress, Welch advocates the ecological and social concerns of twentieth-century Montana (much the same New West agenda as can be found in parts of the West today).

Welch's issue-oriented fiction not only furthers Native American rights and social parity but helps advance the evolution of the Western novel along the lines called for by Larry McMurtry a few years ago and advocated more recently by certain historians and writers of the New West— that is, Welch portrays the issues and tensions of the twentieth-century, post-frontier, urban West.[7] As dramatized by Welch, the New West rises out of the Old, much as a great-grandson absorbs genetically and culturally the family history, the power and gait of a great-grandfather.

In *Winter in the Blood* and *The Death of Jim Loney* Welch began his fictional portrayal of American Indian angst in modern Montana. In those works the nineteenth-century Native American experience makes itself known, primarily as background, in interpolations and flashbacks of certain Blackfeet, Gros Ventre, and Crow Indians. In *Fools Crow* Welch attempts to revisit the ancestral past of some of these modern characters by focusing on the intrusions of whites into the Montana plains country in the 1870s—and the consequent horrors of smallpox, massacre, and deicide. Here Welch presents twentieth-century history only as vision.[8]

One of the linkages of history present, past, and future in these novels and in *The Indian Lawyer* is Welch's various uses of his "Yellow-Calf" characters and namesakes—"warriors" all. In *Winter in the Blood*, the narrator discovers a significant family surprise: Yellow Calf, the old, eccentric blind man nicknamed "Bat Man" who can talk to deer, is really his grandfather, a man who once was proud and courageous and the brunt of no white man's disdain or joke. Yellow Calf, the hunter, had, at the age of sixteen, heroically provided for the narrator's grandmother during the winter Standing Bear, her husband, had been killed.

In *Fools Crow*, the ostracized warrior, Yellow Kidney, mystically knows and anticipates the birth of his grandson, Red Paint's and Fools Crow's son, when he happens across a buffalo cow and her calf the very morning he is to be ambushed and murdered by a vengeful white rancher and his remorseful son. Waiting out a blizzard in a war lodge away from the main camp, Yellow Kidney takes to his death, to the end of his personal history (but also into family history's future), the sight of the special yellow buffalo calf:

> [Yellow Kidney] found himself filled with admiration of the yellow calf—as though its strength and young life somehow embodied all that he had believed in before he became pitiful—and his own life suddenly seemed worth preserving. He thought he might kill the animal anyway, and with the right sacrifices, take a lock of hair for his war bag. He was certain that this calf had been presented to him by Sun Chief as a token of forgiveness. Perhaps the Great Spirit thought he had suffered enough for his transgressions in the Crow camp.
>
> But then the yellow calf lifted his head and looked right at Yellow Kidney and the warrior knew that he could not kill him. Instead, he would take his name away for his grandson. Yellow Calf. A strong name, one that would someday be spoken with fear in the camps of the enemies. (pp. 244–45).

Sylvester Yellow Calf, the protagonist of *The Indian Lawyer*, takes with him, as a new warrior of the New West, this grandfather's wish of Yellow Kidney's; takes with him all the warrior courage of all his fictive and historical namesakes as they reoccur in Welch's novels. Welch, by allusion, even works into his current novel's plotting an ancient war pouch (similar to Yellow Kidney's, mentioned above, and echoing old Grandma's soft-as-old-Bird's-muzzle pouch in *Winter in the Blood*) that once

belonged to Sylvester's great-great-grandfather, the grandfather of Sylvester's grandmother, Mary Bird; the pouch was given to Sylvester by her
during the course of the novel, and relied upon by him as the blackmail
scheme of the Montana State Penitentiary prisoner Jack Harwood, his
wife Patti Ann, and two ex-con partners in crime, Woody Peters and
Robert Fitzgerald, advances to destroy his reputation and his nascent political career.

Sylvester Yellow Calf's status as a new warrior is hard won—whether
facing blackmailers, assimilation and marginality, or himself. Abandoned
by his parents and raised by his grandparents, his battles on the basketball court in high school and at the University of Montana, where he
starred in varsity play, and at Stanford, where he obtained his law degree,
and now, in the novel's historical present of the fall and winter of
1988–1989, all center around his Indianness in a dominant white world.

His political base as a member of the Montana State Prison Parole
Board; his material successes in the prestigious Helena firm of Harrington
and Lohn, first as an associate and then as a partner and vice president;
his announcement as a candidate for Congress on the Democratic ticket;
and his love/sex involvements with the ambivalently tolerant/prejudiced
widow, Shelley Bowers, and with the seductions of Patti Ann Harwood
(encouraged by her husband's revenge and blackmail pressure for parole)—
all of these situations and motives prompt Sylvester to rely on both his
New West/New Indian sophistication and attorney-as-adversary-advocate
training, and on his aboriginal wiles of survival (he is not called "Sly"
gratuitously), on the blessings, protections and power—the old medicines
and mysteries—symbolized by his great-great-grandfather's war pouch.

Mary Bird first gave Sylvester her grandfather's medicine pouch when,
seventeen years back into the history of the novel's present, Sylvester
headed for college and its combat: "[The war pouch] had belonged to her
grandfather and had protected him back in the days when a warrior
needed protection when he went off to battle."9 But Sylvester, youthful
and Americanized, ignores the pouch, and Mary Bird soon finds it tucked
behind some books in his bookcase.

She packs it away in a trunk with his other things. However, as
Sylvester's troubles increase and he returns home to visit his grandparents, she retrieves the pouch and places it on the dresser where her grandson can find it again. This time, again in his childhood room, he not only
notices the pouch but needs it:

> He looked at himself in the mirror above the child's
> dresser. His black hair looked dull and his close-set
> dark eyes were foggy with fatigue. He knocked on the

scratched, sorrel-colored dresser top and noticed the
pouch. He picked it up and felt it. The covering was
soft-tanned hide made hard by the years. The top was
tied shut by a thin yellowing sinew. He held it before
his eyes by the two rawhide strings. It was completely
unadorned and heavier than Sylvester remembered. It
was his great-great-grandfather's war medicine, . . .
He held it to his neck and looked at himself in the mirror again. He tried to see in the mirror a Blackfeet warrior, getting ready to raid the Crow horses, but all he
saw was a man with circles under his eyes, a faint stub-
ble beard on his chin, a man whose only war, skirmish,
actually, was with himself. The new warriors. (p. 165)

Sylvester's status as a new warrior is here dramatized ironically, reflected in his haggard visage and his lifetime of struggle with assimilation. His fears and apprehensions are allayed in part, by the family war
medicine and birthright.

When Mary Bird discovers that her grandson has finally accepted the
war medicine of his grandfathers, Welch balances the earlier mirror visage of Sylvester with that of his grandmother again in front of her grandson's dresser—looking, proudly, old but enduring, into the mirror and all
the way back into Blackfeet history and ancestry: "she stood straight and
saw an old wrinkled face, almost toothless, almost blind, an old Blackfeet
face, laughing at the mirror" (p. 180). The pouch, once historical substance and process—cultural, familial, individual, courageous—is, in
fact, history *as* advocacy.

As Sylvester gathers courage for his decisions to resist blackmail and
fight for his people he looks at the pouch, now hanging from another mirror, this time a mirror in his apartment. He sizes up his historical moment:

He glanced at himself in the mirror. Still the same face,
still Yellow Calf. Blackmail. Maybe it hadn't sunk in
yet. He didn't look like a cornered rat—maybe a tired
rat but definitely not cornered. He glanced at the medicine pouch hanging from a mirror support. He touched
it and he wondered what was in it to make it so hard,
almost like a leather-covered stone. Certainly something as simple as a stone couldn't be the war medicine. It occurred to him that he would never know
what was in the pouch. War medicine was a very pri-
vate matter. Why hadn't it been buried with his great-

great-grandfather? He hadn't asked and his grandmother hadn't volunteered that information. What
had happened to the old Blackfeet warrior? Maybe he
had been killed in a battle and his fellows just had time
to snatch away his medicine before it got into enemy
hands. "There are enemies all around." Wasn't that
part of the scalp dance song? (pp. 293–94)

It is both the history and advocacy implicit in the pouch and in Sylvester's "Indianness" that allow him to make the bid for Congress and
then to return to his childhood home in Browning, closer to his heritage
which he knows he must not escape, must rediscover and advocate in a
scandal-free, stronger run for Congress.

To his credit as a new warrior of old warrior looks and abilities, he
courageously faces down the blackmailers (as he does his own reflection
in the mirror and in the representations of his medicine pouch), foils Harwood's scheme, and in the process wins Patti Ann's love and gratitude. In
returning temporarily to Indian politics and advocacy over the business
and political dealings of his upscale legal practice in Helena, he loses
Shelley and her ambivalence about his Indianness and her whiteness. He
has lost a personal and political battle or two but promises to win the
war. And the war he wages will be to seek and perhaps partially restore
economic, ecological, cultural, and spiritual (especially his own) balance
and harmony. His advocacy, in his mind and in his announcement speech
before the Indian Alliance, resolves "to mount an all-out war on all in-
toxicants on all reservations and Indian communities" (p. 291). The
metaphor is intended and thematically integral to the novel—as story and
history. As basketball player, as attorney, as victim turned aggressor in
Harwood's blackmail attempt, and as politician, advocate, and historian
of his people and himself, Sylvester Yellow Calf is a warrior—a new warrior in a new West.

THE INDIAN LAWYER AND DANCES WITH WOLVES

With the commercial success of *Dances with Wolves* and certain other
popular fictions, such as Tony Hillerman's best-selling Navajo detective
novels and, in a different order, of writings by Leslie Silko, Louise Erdrich,
Michael Dorris, and James Welch, new questions are raised about whether
popular perceptions of Native Americans are merely in a new phase of
older attitudes and assumptions about American ethnicity—or truly part
of the announced New History and what might be called a New Ethnicity. Whether in popular culture or in academe, revisionist views of past

and present images of the United States, Chicanos, Latinos, African Americans, Asian Americans, Native Americans, and, more pointedly, "the American Indian" and "the Indian problem" are coming fast and hard in all the media, causing the coining of one simplistic and confusing slogan after another. It all tends toward a muddle that, above all else, must be resisted, must be thought through and felt through lest we define ourselves only in and through the media.

The commercial slickness and rampant romanticism of an essentially sentimental, celebrity-showcase film like *Dances with Wolves* can be compared instructively with the more complex realism and political concerns of a novel like *The Indian Lawyer*. Both implicitly propagandize the New West, the New Ethnicity—the film by Indianizing an Anglo, the novel by Anglicizing an Indian. But Welch's efforts come across as much more sincere and significant than those of Kevin Costner, the film's director as well as star. As attractive though the idyllic aboriginal life depicted by Costner may be, ultimately Costner's elegiac and millennial efforts may turn out to thwart the nurturing of truly new, more human attitudes about Old Wests and Old Indians.

Why so many teary eyes outside the theater after a showing of *Wolves*? Why such anger and indignation expressed by white audiences against the U.S. Cavalry, their own racial counterparts in the film? Why such empathy by Anglos with Costner's character? It would seem, superficially, that the sentimental response to *Wolves* and its transvaluated characterizations bespeaks a new, mass acceptance of diversity, of Indianness. But *Wolves* simply champions and sentimentalizes one particular tribe of Indian people, made all the more endearing by casting directors and the charismatic actors they chose.

To accept the endorsement of Native Americans as portrayed in *Wolves* requires one to accept the stereotyped negative portrayal of just about every white soldier, wagon driver, and settler in the film. Welch, a Blackfeet/Gros Ventre himself, in *Lawyer* and in his other works (particularly *The Death of Jim Loney*), shows far less "reverse" racism against whites— or, for that matter, against other Indian peoples—than *Wolves* does in its grotesque and hideous portrayals of both white cavalry and Pawnee braves. Ironically, *Wolves* exhibits some of the same limitations of vision for which certain historians of the "New West" criticize the famed (now infamous) father of all historians of the American West, Frederick Jackson Turner. In his arguments for the significance of the American frontier, Turner portrays the North American continent as a destination for white expansionism. Small acknowledgment is made by Turner of the relativity of otherness or of the points of view of other than white Americans.

According to Turner, the American frontier closed in 1890. He saw it as a profound influence on American history—providing motive (call it Manifest Destiny) for the Americanization of European culture, as wave after wave of immigrant settlement surged toward the Pacific. For Turner, the vectors of settlement were two-directional, exclusively East/West. Today we recognize other perceptions of both place and process, of American directionality. Native Americans moved south. Spanish and meztizo moved north. Significant perceptions of North American "destiny" and "frontier," we are now aware, were recorded not just by Euro-Americans and European travelers, but by Native Americans, Mexicans, blacks, and Asians. Clearly, Turner's "wave theory" of inevitable westward progress was ethnocentric, and it is against the grain of Turner's assumptions that *Wolves* and *Lawyer* can be partly measured, at least in historical terms.

When Dunbar arrives at Fort Hays for his assignment, he requests a post on the frontier, saying, "I've always wanted to see the frontier, before it's gone." In the prologue scenes of the film the elegiac nature of the story is established, and the viewer knows what to watch for: ending upon ending upon ending—of Dunbar's primordial, American "macho" dream of western healing, health, and adventure; of the culture and gods of the Sioux he will soon encounter and grow to accept as brothers rather than savages and hostiles to be feared and obliterated; of the tragic federal Indian policy which plays itself out during the course of the film— the crucial Turnerian period from the Civil War to the 1890 "end" of the frontier, the subject of the film's larger goodbye. The historical moment of the film itself is short, a year or so. But the epilogue—flashed on the screen in the same glimmering letters as subtitles that enhance the linguistic reality of the white-Indian encounters by suggesting the variances of Lakota/English, English/Lakota translations—takes us thirteen years into the future when the last band of Sioux surrendered at Fort Robinson, Nebraska, their homes gone, the buffalo killed, their proud horse culture of the plains finished.

Wolves's foreshortened historical view of its "vanishing redman" theme is reflected in its depiction of many minor characters, both white and Indian. As diarist, as writer/soldier, in his speech and in his attitudes, Dunbar is set far apart from the insensitive, boorish frontiersmen—the real savages, such as the belching, farting wagon driver, Timmons, the white teamster who hauls Dunbar and his provisions to Fort Sedgewick, leaves him there amidst the ghostly, dumpy squalor of the deserted post, and then serves as the first instance of Pawnee violence and murder. After watching director Costner's staging of the Pawnee killing and scalping of Timmons; the massacre of the white family of Dunbar's eventual wife, the Sioux adoptee Stands with a Fist; and the ritualized slaughter of a trapped Pawnee raider by the Sioux, I was not surprised that Costner's much publicized membership in the Sioux nation was not matched by the Pawnee. When I discuss *Wolves* with certain Native American viewers, while they like the attempts (albeit patronizing) at "humanizing" Indian culture, almost invariably they lament the portrayal of the "poor Pawnees." Despite possible cinematic justifications such as dramatic tension, the one-sidedness of the film in favor of the Sioux would not be acceptable to past or present Pawnee historians.

Amidst grand vistas and blazing sunsets, Dunbar makes peace with the land and its inhabitants. It's a long series of adjustments meant to dramatize what Dunbar's close friend and surrogate father-in-law, Sioux holy man Kicking Bird, calls "the trail of a good human being," in a speech that never really sidesteps the sappy, in spite of the well-intended theme of developing red/white brotherhood. This is Dunbar's trail throughout the movie: in his friendship with his horse, who is cravenly killed by the most cartoonish company of U.S. Cavalry ever assembled in film or fiction; in his eat-from-my-hand approach to Two Socks, the lone wolf who befriends Dunbar, warns him of approaching dangers, frolics with him on the grasslands, and like Cisco, is shot by the same company of cavalry blackguards; in his rescue of Stands with a Fist as she attempts suicide out of mourning for her Sioux husband's death and her own aloneness; in his love for her and in his friendships with Kicking Bird and with his temporarily fierce Sioux antagonist Winds in His Hair—and, finally, in his participation in the defense of the women, children, and elders from the vengeance of Pawnee raiders.

To Dunbar the Sioux prove anything but savage. They are so eager to laugh, he finds, so devoted to each other, so loyal to family, that he records one simple idea in his journal. Harmony. But set against the insanity of St. David's Field and Fort Hays, the simplicity of a life of harmony is more appealing than convincing. For sure, there is no harmony evidenced by the Anglo buffalo hunters. But what of the Sioux before the incursion of whites? Was their world harmonious? Was it as simple as the film portrays?

Dunbar's harmony is a transvaluated harmony which brings him to new enlightenment, new identity in his first magically real night-sighting of buffalo, the shaggy, archetypal beasts of the prairie; brings him to acceptance with his new-found Sioux brothers, acceptance in his shoulder-to-shoulder stand against the Pawnee, in his naming by those who have witnessed his prairie hijinks with Two Socks. However, the film's lasting value lies in individual scenes and images which will prevail in the viewers' memories, little touchstones, little Wordsworthian spots of time. Viewers will recall the final goodbye—actually a greeting—of Winds in His Hair (who once, in the beginning of the film, had nothing but rancor for whites) as he yells to his new "brother," Dances with Wolves, "I am Winds in His Hair. Do you see that I am your friend. Do you see that I am your friend always." (Would that Columbus and his kin had heard the same voice!) Faults and flaws of *Wolves* notwithstanding, in these human images, these moving pictures, the new, revisionist phase of imaging and imagining ourselves *in* and *as* American Indians will, we hope, bring us all closer to the new era of ethnic and cultural awareness.

In *The Indian Lawyer*, Welch does true service to the cause of humanizing images of Native Americans by portraying, of all things, a "successful" American Indian—in touch with both white and Native American cultures. His journey toward becoming a good human being is, in reverse of Dunbar's, an excursion into Anglo politics. Welch places his protagonist on the streets, in the offices, in the homes, and in the beds of the white establishment—paleface and redskin living and working, loving and hating, together. "You mean Indians go to law school?" "Get high paying jobs?" "Run for office?" "Lust and are lusted after?" This is the stuff of a new kind of frontier fiction about a truly bold and brave new frontier.

Welch wears his Indianness matter of factly, as he does his Americanness. For more than twenty years his books have been extending the parameters of the Western novel, the new ethnicity, just as Costner has attempted to revitalize the Western film. Welch has made each of his novels a reflection of the twentieth-century realignment of American attitudes toward Indianness, place (social and geographical), and literature, and especially of the roles of oral tradition and myth, of white and Indian political and sexual encounters.

Welch's role as chronicler of the changing West has not been simply passive. His novels have also helped foster the cultural and political agendas that are now transforming the idea and the reality of Native Americans, ethnicity, and the West. *Fools Crow*, Welch's version of post-Civil War Indian/white relations, could very well have served Costner's purposes as a much more profound revisionist script, a new look into, in this instance, Blackfeet and Crow as human beings in search of, momentarily attaining but finally losing, "harmony." In *Fools Crow*, the nemesis is much more encompassing than the stupidity of federal policies, the U.S. Cavalry, and massacre, though those are part of the story; it includes smallpox and religious and social betrayals.

In *The Indian Lawyer*, Welch offers readers an especially intriguing plot and "hero." To the conventions of the captivity narrative, the cowboy/Indian Western, the mountain man saga, the U.S. Cavalry case study of brutality and abuse, Indian love song and initiation story, Welch adds new elements of crime story and environmental and ethnic themes and techniques—a recipe that squeezes out and blends, spices up and cooks the juices of Whitman's old democratic soup: "Simmering, simmering, simmering."

Welch says that he got the idea for *Lawyer* from his own experiences as a member of Montana's Parole Board. Welch's alter-ego, and Indian counterpart to Costner's Lieutenant John Dunbar, is Indian attorney Sylvester Yellow Calf, a man who, in the course of his visits to Montana State Prison and his issuing of "establishment" verdicts as a member of the parole board, crosses a smooth but vengeful white convict, Jack Harwood. Old West racism is triggered, and trouble for Yellow Calf begins. Harwood, criminally inclined as he is, never becomes as campy in his villainy and vulgarity as do the ass-wiping, face-kicking soldiers of *Wolves*. Welch reserves some of that for even more hardened convicts in the novel, many of them Indians.

Harwood, more hardened by the prison experience than he first realizes, sets his seductive wife, Patti Ann, after Yellow Calf. Harwood, of course, doesn't allow for Yellow Calf's good looks and erotic attractiveness to his lonely wife. And Welch handles the red/white sexual unions in the book much more forthrightly than is seen in *Wolves*, where the marriage of white Stands with a Fist to a Sioux is completely off camera. Dunbar's sexual scenes with Stands with a Fist are really white making love to white—a kind of reawakening of white lovemaking civilities combined with initiations into soft "savage" sex.

The double-identity, loyalty-betrayal, red man/white woman turns of plot and character that face Patti Ann and Sylvester make for some both steamy and scary complications. Peters and Fitzgerald, as Indian/white homosexual lovers, also afford an intriguing variation on other taboo relationships—in the evolving tradition of white/Indian lovers in American fiction and film. The more politically correct portrayal of such relationships in *Wolves* is, of course, resolved by a white man trying to become Indian marrying a white woman who long ago almost became Indian.

Not only must Yellow Calf sort out his real relationship with Pattie Ann and foil Harwood and his gang, he must also wrestle with his successes as an attorney in the relatively upscale white society of Helena, Montana. Very much a man of his times, in which lip service is paid to "racial diversity," Yellow Calf finds himself sought after by a senator's daughter, Shelly Bowers, and regional and national power players in the Democratic Party. Subsequent "laying on of hands" (sexual and political) threatens to compromise Sylvester's allegiance to his Native American birthright. At risk are the old ways of his grandparents, of Lena Old Horn, his erstwhile high-school counselor and earth-mother object of his past erotic yearnings, his quest for the female ideal—a search made all the more illusive by his parental abandonment. In layering Yellow Calf's past identity on his present one in the final third of the novel, Welch masterfully argues for the truism that success means acceptance of one's past and one's cultural roots which stabilize later cultural assimilations. In a more subliminal way *Wolves* advances the same theme in that Dunbar must leave his Sioux brothers and return to the larger, empowered white political world, seek out the leaders, and tell his and the Indians' story.

Faced with the harassments of Harwood and company, the siren songs of Patti Ann and Shelley, and the lingering claims of his Indian ancestry, Sylvester Yellow Calf must try to reclaim the power of his great-great-grandfather. Returning to the reservation, he sees how he must incorporate the old verities of loyalty to land and kin in the new Indian agenda. It is an agenda that must include his assimilated "whiteness," as well as his rooted Indianness. To become a successful politician in Montana and in the nation, he must revive the old warrior ways of his ancestors. And Welch dramatizes this nicely in intimate ways whereby Yellow Calf reclaims his old childhood and his incremental manly courage through repossessing his family amulet. This New Warrior/New Ethnicity theme is one of the most pervasive and convincing themes in the novel, one which in the Welch canon changes heretofore antiheroic characters into heroic ones and offers a counterpoint of future promise to past strains of elegy and apocalypse.

Far from any sentimentalized advocacy of happy hunting grounds restored or of simplistic racial blame and accusation, Welch's protagonist in *Lawyer* argues for a new political and social agenda founded in his reclaiming of old democratic principles. Like Whitman before him, and like Costner in his cinematic imaging, Welch affirms yet again the belief advocated in the founding of our nation. What else is the New History, the New Ethnicity, other than the old democracy? Whether as historians or novelists, scriptwriters, directors, producers or publishers, actors or characters, audiences or critics, minorities or majorities, white people become Indian, or people of color become white, that is the agenda which faces us more urgently now than when *Dances with Wolves* and *The Indian Lawyer* were first released. When will the New America learn from the old? When will prejudice and hatred, anger and violence, when will war, of whatever kind and scope, resolve into racial and social, cultural and ecological harmony?

LISTENING TO RAY A. YOUNG BEAR

In my dream-eye came her words and reminded
me of a story i once fell asleep to.
— "These Horses Came," Ray A. Young Bear

Like so many Native American singers and seekers, be they real or fictive,
Ray A. Young Bear charges the present with the sounds of the past and
creates new memories for himself and for his readers—Indian and non-
Indian alike. Such paradoxes are inherent in the poetic process generally
and more particularly in those "spots of time" seen so often by Words-
worth and the romantics. And the poetic process is very much on Young
Bear's mind; this and what he calls, in one of his poems, "the act of remembering,"[1] is the subject here—and intended in part as introductory
insofar as no critical essays on Young Bear's work had appeared when
this essay was first published.[2] What is worth considering is how, through
imagery and idea, one soon senses in reading Young Bear's poetry a voice
that hears, echoes, and sees shadows of what the speaker, and behind him
the poet, wants to say. The poet's hope is to restate in written rather than
oral language what was seen and heard and sung long before. In this
sense, Young Bear's words are those of dreams and memories.

Richard Hugo wrote in 1973, "Ray A. Young Bear is magic. He writes
as if he lived 10,000 years ago in a tribe whose dialect happens to be modern English."[3] Although Young Bear has published in dozens of journals,
is the author of numerous books, and is included in just about all an-
thologies of contemporary American Indian poetry,[4] no one has improved
Hugo's description of Young Bear's impact on readers. Most commenta-
tors go little beyond "notes on contributors" and biographical information like the following early sketch by Duane Niatum in *Carriers of the
Dream Wheel*: "Ray A. Young Bear was born in Tama, Iowa, in 1950. His
tribe is Sauk and Fox of Iowa, better known as the Mesquakies. He has

been writing since 1966 and says he begins by thinking in his native Mesquaki [*sic*] and then translating [*sic*] his thoughts into English."[5] Necessary and helpful as these introductions are in determining such things as where Young Bear has studied (Claremont College, Grinnell College, the State University of Iowa, and the University of Northern Iowa), it is through the poetry, of course, that Young Bear tells of his life— past, present, and future.

In Fred McTaggart's *Wolf that I Am*, the ursine figure of James North affords an intriguing but oblique portrait of Ray Young Bear that takes us somewhat closer to his poetry. McTaggart, in his informal study, characterizes North as an Iowa City poet, just returned from California, who serves as mentor and culture bridge in McTaggart's search for the Red Earth People as he shuttles between Mesquakie Settlement and the university collecting and pondering Mesquakie myths and writing his doctoral dissertation, which is the basis of *Wolf*.

One account of James North as Mesquakie singer provides an opportune introduction to Young Bear's poetry as an act of listening and remembering. McTaggart describes his personal response to James North's singing: "I could never separate James's voice from that of the other men, and, of course, I could not understand the words. But when I listened closely and let myself relax I could hear many voices—the voices of the birds and the beasts of the universe, singing in unison."[6] Such a response is reminiscent of the "magic" Hugo speaks of in relation to Young Bear; the mysterious voices heard by McTaggart in North's singing can also be heard in Young Bear's poetry. And in the translation from Indian to English, from oral to written word you hear Young Bear (as he indicates to Duane Niatum in *Carriers of the Dream Wheel*) saying with James North, "I hear the poem in Indian . . . then I have to translate it into English. It is very difficult because there are some words that you just don't have and there are others that just can't be translated."[7] And it is memory, as complicated as that is in relation to dream and the psychology of creation and transcendence, that motivates and shapes Young Bear's poetry.

Where memory ends and dream begins for Young Bear is difficult to determine; however, tracing causality is perhaps not all that important because they blend continuously within a given poem and from poem to poem. For the moment, suffice it to say that memory and dream work as both structure and process. One exceptionally beautiful and successful poem which reflects how this works is a willed journey into the past, to more glorious and healthy days, as a means of demonstrating to facile-minded, pseudo-Indian types what the world and mind of the old people really were—"really were" in Young Bear's dream-eye. The poem is an angry demonstration against the trendy poet, editor, and reader; it is a poem written, to quote its final lines (in its first appearance in *Poetry Northwest*), "in disgust and in response / to indian-type poetry / written by whites / published in a mag / which has rejected me / too many times."[8]

Because the poem's own language is too enjoyable to miss, some extended quotation is necessary. The poem opens in the present but with a longing for the past—a longing that will be fulfilled by the transporting power of listening to memory and dream:

> *you know we'd like to be there*
> *standing beside our grandfathers*
> *being ourselves*
> *without the frailty*
> *and insignificance of the worlds*
> *we suffer and balance*
> *on top of now*
> *unable to detect which to learn*
> *or which to keep from*
> *wearing the faces*
> *of our seasonal excuses*
> *constantly lying to each other*
> *and ourselves about just how much*
> *of the daylight*
> *we understand*
> *we would be there: (p. 18)*

At this point, after the disconnection and suffering, the lies and blindness of the present, the ironies of daylight misunderstanding and seasonal excuses, the poet-speaker collectively transcends time and stands behind his grandfathers in authentic balance of mind—with the clarity of vision offered by the darkness of myth and the approaching sacred autumn. It is a magical mind-spirit journey, a memory of the blood, a dream, at least in process, like those of Coleridge's great conversational lyrics. Once with the grandfathers, the speaker would be in the past . . .

> *with the positions of our minds*
> *bent towards the autumn fox*
> *feasts*
> *feeling the strength and prayer*
> *of the endured sacred human tests*
> *we would set aside the year's*
> *smallpox dead*
> *whole and complete*

with resignation
like the signs from the four legs
of our direction
standing still
sixty years back in time
breathing into the frosted lungs
of our horses the winter blessings
of our clan gods
through dependence
they would carry our belongings
and families to the woodlands
of eastern iowa to hunt our food
separate and apart
from the tribe
following and sometimes using
the river to cleanse the blood
from our daughters and wives
now knowing that far into
our lives we'd be the skulls
of their miscarriages
as a result: (pp. 18–19)

The effect of such a dream is eerily heightened by the omnipresence of the speaker's voice, knowing that the future of those populating his memory provide his own present; it is the epic, synchronic voice of heritage and race. And just as the larger structures juxtapose or, in terms of the poem, "balance" day and night, knowing and not knowing, present and past, so life imagery (breathing, cleansing, strength) balances the imagery of death. Moreover, natural death ("the year's / smallpox dead") counters spiritual death ("we'd be the skulls / of their miscarriages").

The third section continues as a mystical non sequitur deeper into religion and ritual with the greater prominence of the clan gods. All in a dream world where and when, as a result of following and using the holy river water,

the salamander would paralyze
our voice and hearing
under instruction
our sons the mutes would darken
their bodies with ash and we'd assist
them erect sweatlodges with canvas
water plants fire and poles

from the river
the scent of deer and geese
the hiss of medicine
against the heated rocks
belief would breathe into their bodies
camouflage and invisibility
somewhere an image of a woman's hand
would lunge out from the window
of a longhouse
and it would grab from our fingers
the secret writings of a book
describing to the appointee
the method of entering
the spirit and body
of a turkey
to walk at night in suspension
above the boundaries of cedar incense
to being this line of witchcraft
travelling in various
animal forms
unaware of the discrepancy
that this too is an act of balance
a recurring dream of you
being whole and complete
sending the glint of your horns
into the great distances
of the gods
acquainting yourself with ritual
and abandonment of self-justification
to realize there is a point
when you stop being a people
sitting somewhere and reading
the poetry of others come out easily
at random
unlike yours which is hard to write
to feel yourself stretch
beyond limitation
to come here and write this poem
about something no one
knows about
no authority to anything (pp. 19–20)

With the reentry into the present, into the "here" of writing the poem, the memory and the dream are ended even though the words of the poem and the vision of the poet's dream-eye remain as an interlude of the imagination, a testimonial to the kinship of art and witchcraft, poetry and life, memory and dream paralleled metaphorically as "an act of balance / a recurring dream of you / being whole and complete / sending the glint of your horns / into the great distances / of the gods."

In the various ways of memory and dream, in images of violence and tranquillity, longing and fulfillment, the grotesque and the beautiful, Young Bear's poetry takes us to the world of the old ones, set against the struggles of a grandson trying to "listen," and to write "about something no one / knows about / no authority to anything." McTaggart suggests James North's (Young Bear's) grandmother is at the very heart of his poetry. And in a sense, she is the embodiment of memory, appearing as personage and metaphor, a listening presence, throughout his works.

In "Before Leaving Me, the Poem: Eagle Butte and Black River Falls" Young Bear's grandmother accompanies him and his wife to Black River Falls, Wisconsin, for Memorial Day singing and celebration with numerous tribes and people. In the midst of the crowd, feeling lost and disoriented when familiar faces turn away, it is grandmother who gives stabilizing advice and turns the poet's thoughts poignantly inward, augmenting his recurring responses to the Wisconsin landscape:

> . . . *we kept staring at each other*
> *when most of the motels rejected us.*
> *over hamburgers and coke, my grandmother*
> *spoke, "some people try to hide their lives*
> *as long as they can, but we see them*
> *and help them when members of their family*
> *pass away. it doesn't work to feel important."*
> *somehow I knew it was the same for me.*
> *i was no better. but for a moment*
> *it came in the form of a small whirlwind,*
> *rushing in my dream in search of pinetrees,*
> *waiting for me to be uplifted and shaken*
> *from the fog, to find myself within the cracks*
> *of the whispering walls, undergoing test*
> *upon test, wondering whether or not*
> *we'd ever be together like this again.*
> *the three of us, pressed on by the people*
> *around us to go our own distorted ways.*[9]

As seen also in "In Disgust and in Response," listening to memory and dream, like the wisdom of a grandparent, brings at least temporary balance and stability for Young Bear.

In "Four Songs of Life," one of his more widely anthologized poems, Young Bear speaks in the voices of both old and young about the despair and comfort of memory and dream. In the first song, a young man, reminiscent of the husband-grandson in "Before Leaving Me," remains empty and alienated, lamenting a kind of cultural amnesia:

> *the blue rain*
> *quiet in feelings*
> *losing*
> *nothing—showing no one*
> *that i am cold*
> *in this*
> *earth*
> *singing different songs*
> *i never heard*
> *from the same people*
> *unable*
> *to*
> *create or remember*
> *their own*
> *songs to keep*[10]

In the second song, continuing the lament, we see the reasons for each sterility and forgetfulness when we hear in an old man's song the notes of guarded selfishness:

> *i remember well*
> *my people's*
> *songs.*
> *i will not reveal*
> *to anyone*
> *that i*
> *know these songs.*
> *it was*
> *intended for me*
> *to keep*
> *them in secrecy*
> *for they are now*
> *mine to die with me.*[11]

But in the third song the tonalities change as lament modulates toward anthem as "one who realized," an appointee, recounts a past invocation:

i sang
to the warm sun
and cold moon
this morning
and offered
myself
to the land
and gods
for them
to
teach
me
the old
hard ways
of living
all over again[12]

The fourth song ends the sequence in a lullaby of community and union sung at a moment when "he was approached" and comforted through "listening," through memory and dream:

a time
in sadness
within
the night
holding me
and comforting me.
here i am
being
taught
to be
a man
with life
and old sacred
songs to guide
me
and love me forever.[13]

Young Bear's act of remembering, his poetry, is an attempt to be guided and loved by life and the old sacred songs. Happiness for the poet is indeed in the memories and dreams of the imagination and these themes carry on throughout Young Bear's writing. Even at the age of twenty-seven, he identifies mystically with the old ones, and in poems like "The Last Dream" the reader senses that the old singer-healer is an analog of Young Bear himself; though he speaks in third person he is also speaking about himself—present, past, and future—and the restorative, healing power of words and listening in the face of death, "the last dream, / the grandfather of all / dream."[14]

It is through memory and dream that the "student of dreams" encountered in "A Pool of Water, a Reflection of a Summer" learns the old, hard, whole ways and avoids the inarticulate awkwardness of the contemporary, white world. The doubleness of Young Bear's old and young, grandparent and grandson, master and student self is keenly seen in this poem, which dramatizes Young Bear as both a keeper and a sharer of dreams in search of inspiration—symbolized in a long series of poems by various fantasy fish. Consider the mythic fullness of the opening stanza:

> from the very beginning of the summer,
> we sat beside the brown river while it flooded.
> we imagined great suspended fish under the rapids
> and foam, taking the bait into their mouths
> and sending the vibrations of their power
> through our lines into our hands.[15]

And then, this shift to another, even more allegorical narrative level:

> and the man who gave away dreams died along
> with his songs. his memory. the clans.
> there was a man who sat beside him,
> a student who boasted about his mental
> capabilities of remembering the songs
> and their sequence. how he could outsing
> the old man.

But such boasting is short-lived because the word is not easily passed on, the giant fish are not easily caught in reality or in the mind, and the young listener/dreamer is often left with aspiration rather than inspiration:

> later on, the student of dreams will sit in silence.
> no songs will come into his mind. it will be awkward.
> he will only sit there and remember the man who gave
> away dreams.

Oversimplifying the magic, Young Bear's poetry deals with the struggles of a young American Indian poet to re-create in memory and dream a heritage of life and myth removed from him by social and cultural forces beyond his immediate control. In the mere act of listening and remembering, however, Young Bear is influencing those forces for himself, his people, and American poetry. He remains in the vanguard of today's indigenous poets, proving with a vengeance Vine Deloria's belief that "in the poetry of the modern Indian we find a raging sense of having been and a desperate pronouncement of future being, an effort beyond nobility that calls for recognition of the humanity and nationality of Indian existence."[16]

MESQUAKIE SINGER

Listening to Ray A. Young Bear's poetry isn't easy. His songs are sad ones, whether love song or lament, and the "meaning" is obscure even for modern poetry. In addition, most of his poems are long (many of his early ones run over ten pages in manuscript) and evidence the typically modern non sequitur or stream of consciousness psychology or technique.[17] One commentator refers to Young Bear's poetry as fascinating, troubling, surrealistic.[18] In part, the difficulty for non-Native American readers is cultural. Young Bear is an Indian hearing his words in Mesquakie (so he says), writing in English, but not especially for a non-Indian audience. One senses that Young Bear is singing to himself and to his people—Sac and Fox, living and dead. So, in part, the difficulty in Young Bear's poetry is due to the autobiographical aspects of his work: details of his domestic life; his love for his wife, his grandmother, and other old ones; his alienation from white literary, academic, and middle-class culture; his ambivalence and sometimes anger at white culture; his fighting, fishing, hunting; his nightmares and visions; his maturation as a man and a poet; and the intermingling of it all in mind, memory, and sensation. Partly too the difficulty is one of listening to the persona and to Young Bear, distinguishing Young Bear from someone like William Badger, for example, when that or some other clan voice is assumed. In this sense the difficulty is stylistic, discovering the ways Young Bear uses to dramatize himself, listening for his changing voices.

Even so, faithful listeners to Young Bear soon come to know that in the style, in the sadness and difficulty of his voicings, is the pleasure. In a sense, the pleasurable problems encountered in listening to Young Bear are no different from those which always face readers of richly textured imagistic, lyric poetry.

Attention can profitably be directed to how the singer-poet becomes the audience-listener and how the audience-listener becomes the singer. I use the term *singer* with intentional ambiguity. The colloquial speaker in Young Bear's poetry is also a singer in the American Indian, ceremonial sense of the word—one who chants the old songs or at least attempts to learn them. And there is as much music as there is musing, more singing than one might at first suspect, in Young Bear's poetry.

I will comment on three poems about the old songs and their new singing. Listen first to part of a long prose poem—untitled and unpublished—regrettably, but necessarily fragmented here, about the naming and growth of William Badger and his struggle to retain in song the old beliefs in a world of dissipation and disbelief:

> *the marijuana was handed to him. he smoked it like he*
> *was*
> *told. he began to feel extremely guilty for the times he*
> *missed the dances. nothing on earth could ever replace*
> *their occurrence. he always sang the songs of the*
> *dances*
> *in his head:*
> *never leave us*
> *the wave over the river*
>
> *swim and make the bottom*
> *glow*
>
> *i remember the ribbon*
> *which ties my existence*
> *and whole dependence*
> *to your existence*
>
> *ever since the day he chose to stay home, he went over*
> *the songs*
> *continually. his father praised his memory years before*
> *when*
> *they began to sing them. it never bothered him to go*
> *through a*
> *day with the songs alive and humming the warmth*
> *through his body*
> *and mind while he was busy with his daily tasks. they*
> *planted*
> *themselves deep within him.*

The dancing and the singing which William Badger, always hearing and singing, carries with him, and which the marijuana, with its odor of remembered medicine roots, causes to surface in his mind and inner ear, appear as the river wave; as the song and motion of the water and the glowing river bottom; as a ribbon, metaphorically tied to the river of life and the sacred river rituals of the spirit fish that carry the spirit of his name—part of the myth of the birthfish that William narrates elsewhere in the poem. The change which we hear William hearing and repeating as part of his very blood's being is nothing less than a song of life, a song of beauty's way. In singing is life, we hear; in the silence is death.

Merle Brown's remarks on what is involved in comprehending poetry may shed some light on Young Bear's work:

> Poetry is difficult to access not because of its special
> qualities of autonomy and experiential vitality, but be-
> cause it is listened to as it is spoken, heard critically as
> it is expressed, read as it is being written: it comes to
> the reader twice-told. The poet always listens to him-
> self as part of the expressive act that is his poem, and
> that listening becomes an essential part of the com-
> pleted poem. It is never fused into the expressiveness
> of the act of the poem's making, but continues to be in
> dramatic relationship with that expressiveness.[19]

Certainly Young Bear's literally listening to the old songs as he writes a new one seems to be "in dramatic relationship with his expressiveness." Insofar as the reader-listener can listen to Young Bear listening to himself (poet and persona), and can empathetically hear if not become a singer-listener with Young Bear, "understanding" for the reader becomes a process as much as it is an end; which is to say that one senses Young Bear is always involved with trying to understand his own act of writing poetry whereby his poem becomes that self-same attempt. As such, Young Bear's singing becomes a kind of salvation, a way of religiously immersing himself again in the creative continuity of his culture.

To be sure, the theme of continuity—fish to water, person to time and place, singer to song, song to listener—is extremely important to Young Bear, becoming inextricably part of the song, the singing, the listening, the word, communication. In "A Pool of Water, a Reflection of a Summer," Young Bear sings about the need to pay homage to an elder, a teacher of singers, who has just died, but

> *being afraid to see his still presence,*
> *we fished that day. this wasn't the first for me.*
> *it was a time to replace reality with the arbors*

of a hunt. the sand from the beach drifted pebble
by pebble into the rushing river.

once when i went to a funeral for two people,
i bid them farewell in english. i wanted to stop
and start over. i felt stupid as i walked away
from them, but the line kept moving.
many wanted to put this day behind them.

in the hot misty haze with our barefeet and backs,
we heard what sounded like bees swarming from tree
to tree. at times it sounded like talk and then singing.
i abandoned the idea of nightfishing.
completely forgot about the fish
who had broken our 20 pound test
three times.

Here Young Bear is the "I" who finds English so inadequate for saying goodbye, for the reverent singing times such as death. Thus, "a pool of water" becomes Young Bear's way of starting over again, of not putting the day behind him; his way of reviving the songs, if not word for word and sequence for sequence, then at least in process—as a means of avoiding the awkwardness that resides in sterile words, in silence, when "no songs will come into his mind," when he can only aspire to give away dreams himself, like the dead elder to whom he was "student."

Now listen to Young Bear as he projects himself into the sorrowful role of a young singer who yearns to sing the old songs of his beginnings but with little encouragement from, rather surprisingly, a disbelieving elder. But Young Bear sings in spite of him. In the face of disappointments like the one dramatized here, Young Bear is resolved to "carry the songs." Listen to Ray A. Young Bear, Mesquakie singer. Listen as the song carries on and on . . . , making us too the carrier of its melody and voice, the keepers of its words.

now the two old men have nothing
to fear from each other

one is dead
the other still leads
the long arduous
prayers

there's no time
to make apologies
anymore

no time to verbally
correct the older man
who sits above
the triangle

he's gone also
i don't think anyone
wants to admit
that the songs
are lost

the four walls
support the believers

the last one
criticizes the believers
within the four walls

many think he has
to be right
he
above all others
is closer to our beginnings

he questions who
of the young will carry
on with the songs

he says
no one will

he says he is the only
one

whats the use
of believing in anything
when there isn't
encouragement

one would think that
if someone leads
what he thinks
will be the last
religion

he should help
as much as possible

afterall
isn't that why
he adopted this purpose

and of the young
who sit with him
in his prayers
when they were told

none of them would
carry the songs

i wonder how they
felt at the day's end

Keeper of the words, carrier of the songs, Young Bear continues on the poet's path of truth and beauty. And listening, the reader, in affirmation, anticipates day's beginning.

WINTER OF THE SALAMANDER

Ray Anthony Young Bear's poetry began appearing with growing frequency in journals and reviews during the 1970s. *Winter of the Salamander,* Young Bear's first book of poems, the culmination of his 1970s apprenticeship, confirmed his importance. Almost upon publication, *Winter of the Salamander* (1980) became one of the half-dozen or so absolutely essential books to read (especially for non-Native Americans) for a no-holds-barred, angry, violent, grotesque, beautiful, loving look at the place and persona of an Indian poet's experience in a dominantly Anglo-American world. As such, it was a major revelation.

Like Tiger Salamander of his Iowa home, however, Young Bear and his work go more or less unnoticed by readers outside academic Indian circles. In a special sense *Winter of the Salamander, The Invisible Musician,* and *Black Eagle Child* need to be more widely read.

To read *Winter of the Salamander,* Young Bear's first volume of poetry, is to know the anguish of "otherness," the mistake of prejudice and stereotyping. To read *Winter of the Salamander* is to see a man and an "Indian" confessing the most intimate and honest of thoughts and feelings. It is to know confusion and enlightenment, to follow a self search and a family search, to hear a proclamation of me in relation to you, now—and then. It is to encounter myth and the mundane. It is to experience utterly different yet hauntingly familiar words and images. It is to know the Mesquakies and everyman, everyplace. It is to see animals and humans in the strangest, most magical of metamorphoses. It is to be happy and sad in front of a windowed, but expansive view of the "thing-ness" and alienation of America.

Representative of the important revelations attendant to reading *Winter of the Salamander* are two poems that first appeared in *The American Poetry Review* in the spring of 1978: "I Can Still Picture the Caribou," and "For the Rain in March: The Blackened Hearts of Herons." Long poems even for Young Bear, they run to nearly twenty pages in Part Four of *Winter of the Salamander*.

The persona in both poems speaks in the first person of a world gone awry, of distortions where nothing fits, least of all the confessional speaker of the poems. Both poems turn from association to association, from one reality to another, day-awakening to daydream and fantasy, from conscious to unconscious, from pedestrian to sublime diction and imagery. The animals in the titles of both poems function as oblique objective correlatives for the state of mind and spirit of the persona himself, who, in an ecological plight like the Alaskan caribou, evokes the cry, "let's save the fucking things." Only in mind and memory can the victimized and, by implication, doomed speaker

> . . . *still picture the caribou,*
> *running alongside a green moist hill*
> *with its antlers raised up towards the sky.*
> *with clouds, everywhere.*

The picture of that glorious escape, that proud, utopian freedom seems but a passing hope for the surgeon-surrounded patient with one lung, the vine-strangled junked car "passenger," the buffalo, bears, seals, and seagulls who, in kinship with the speaker, face no future. The future, like the present, holds nothing like the wholeness of the past, a time when

> *seventy-five years ago, our places*
> *were probably filled with dance*
> *and constant prayer.*
> *breath made of the day's*
> *offering instead of alcohol.*

The future is merely mutilation, symbolized by "a legless and headless man."

Clichés of marginality aside, in these poems the reader (particularly the non-Native American reader) encounters the reflection, the visage of himself or herself as very much a part of the victimizing process—in collective and individual terms. This dynamic dual perception is introduced in the title of Part Four of the book: "The Sound He Makes—The Sound I Hear," and is reinforced in the parade of "persons" in "For the Rain in March." Observe the comically grotesque cigar-smoking badger who rams pieces of burning wood into his eyes in front of the hallucinating speaker who is used to seeing such things as "the struggling / black and yellow / spotted body of a salamander / freeing itself from a young / girl's womb," "a hand reaching into hot boiling / water," and

> . . . *the small hands*
> *of a toad examining my round*
> *face*
> *the hammock moved within*
> *the toad's breath and when he*
> *walked away boils grew over the places*
> *where it had touched me . . .*

In these images the speaker has seen reflections of himself, a self in his "life ahead," certain only that he "will never know who I actually am / nor will the woman who lives with me / know me or herself or the children / we want." The longhaired rednecks whom the speaker fantasizes shooting with his automatic pistol, the fat redhead "pig" policeman whose brains the speaker envisions splattering everywhere with a well-placed .38 slug behind the ear, the poets who think they know all about Indianness in claiming a "good 64th" degree of Indian blood—in these, as well as in the bullet-ridden "blackened heart of herons" and the "dismembered body of a girl / scattered for a quarter of a mile," are the darker, id-buried, marrow-deep horrors not just of Young Bear's violent imaginings but of humanity's cruelties inflicted upon itself and on nature at large.

Young Bear's importance as an artist, a poet, and an American Indian is ultimately in his rendering of these primitive and shocking perceptions. With *Winter of the Salamander* Ray A. Young Bear proves himself a savage poet in something of the sense of Aldous Huxley's Savage in *Brave New World*: a keeper of importance—the importance of knowing pleasure and pain, of feeling the power of language, of the word.

Surrounded by savage voices of other kinds, *Winter of the Salamander* is a "first" book very much worthy of wider recognition, and Young Bear's indigenous voice is an important one for all to hear and heed.

THE INVISIBLE MUSICIAN

Richard Hugo was right. Young Bear speaks with a voice thousands of years old. In part this is attributable to Young Bear's conceiving the world poetically—imagistically, rhythmically. In part it is attributable to Young Bear's bilingualism, his ability to think of his poetry in his ancient Algonquin tongue and speak it or translate it into the accessibilities of English.

In *The Invisible Musician* as in *Winter of the Salamander*, the effect is a transportation that allows modern non-Indian readers to catch a glimmering of pure *Word*, pure language, in a kind of atemporal, projected, eternalized moment.

Such profundity in Young Bear's verse is often itself invisible. Many of his poems are five and six pages long—and divided into intriguingly complex parts; some poems, especially his Mesquakie love songs, are quite short—and disarmingly simple. Here is one such song:

Ne to bwa ka na,	My pipe,
bya te na ma wi ko;	hand it over to me;
ne to bwa ka na	my pipe,
bya te na ma wi ko	hand it over to me;
ne to bwa ka na	my pipe,
bya te na ma wi ko	hand it over to me.
Ne a ta be swa	I shall light and inhale
a ta ma	tobacco
sha ske si a.	for the single woman.
Ne to bwa ka na,	My pipe,
bya te na ma wi ko.	hand it over to me.[20]

In the beauty of its tribal sound and rhythms, this "Mesquakie Love Song" sings out strong and vibrant, as if from some settlement pow-wow or some more ancient, now encoded and repeated love yearning and resolve.

Such ancient updatings find their complements throughout *The Invisible Musician* in contemporary dirges. In "*Wa ta se Na ka mo ni*, Viet Nam Memorial," a poem that reiterates the volume's title, Young Bear bridges the ancient and the modern:

Last night when the yellow moon
of November broke through the last line
of turbulent Midwestern clouds,
a lone frog, the same one
who probably announced
the premature spring floods,
attempted to sing.
Veterans' Day, and it was
sore throat weather.
In reality the invisible musician

reminded me of my own doubt.
The knowledge that my grandfathers
were singers as well as composers—
one of whom felt the simple utterance
of a vowel made for the start
of a melody—did not produce
the necessary memory or feeling
to make a Wa ta se Na ka mo ni,
Veteran's Song.
All I could think of
was the absence of my name
on a distant black rock.
Without this monument
I felt I would not be here.
For a moment I questioned
why I had to immerse myself
in country, controversy, and guilt;
but I wanted to honor them.
Surely, the song they presently
listened to along with my grandfathers
was the ethereal kind which did not stop.[21]

So too is the music, the poetry of Young Bear, the "ethereal kind" that links us all to the old verities.

THE FACEPAINT NARRATIVES

Black Eagle Child (*Black Eagle Child: The Facepaint Narratives*, 1992) is a transitional work in Young Bear's progress as a poet and a writer, a work that synthesizes much of his past writing while simultaneously making giant strides along new pathways.

Now in midlife as a person and in midcareer as a writer, Young Bear offers us and himself an imaginative account of his making as an artist. *Black Eagle Child*, published in the Iowa Series in North American Autobiography, most certainly belongs to that tradition of "portraits of an artist as a young man"—but with what a powerful difference!

For here in "The Facepaint Narratives" of Young Bear's dramatization of himself as Edgar Bearchild—resident of the Black Eagle Child Settlement and of the beautiful, crazy, angst-ridden world of his own darkly humorous mind and heart—author and reader see and feel what it's like to love and to do battle with an aboriginal heritage in a modern world.

Just as Edgar Bearchild and his buddies, Ted Facepaint and Junior

Pipestar, are only distancing disguises for Young Bear himself, so is Black Eagle Child a renaming of the Mesquakie Settlement near Tama, Iowa. In the absurdist world of Bearchild and Facepaint and their acquaintances, the Settlement elementary school becomes the Weeping Willow Elementary School and the nearby south-central town of What Cheer becomes Why Cheer, academic home of first-love Dolores Fox-King, and the Why Cheer High School Indian girls' club.

Pathos and passion abound in Black Eagle Child Settlement and its environs. These set-aside acres of the Settlement are for all purposes forgotten by the bigwigs in Des Moines and demeaned by do-gooders who devise schemes to give all tribal members a few thousand dollars for a sociological experiment to see what effects "wealth" may bring to the "Indians."

Young Bear's satirical thrusts spare few in either the white or the Native American culture as he crosses between the two worlds, writing not so much as a "marginal man" but rather as a seer and shaman whose biting, atavistic images slice away all cant.

Edgar's anger is apparent throughout, but nowhere more trenchantly than in his long eulogy to the returning ghost of his companion singer and reveler, Pat "Dirty" Red Hat, whose drunken death in a car wreck is relegated to mere state statistics—money unwisely granted, confirmation of a test-case hypothesis. It is during Edgar's stint as a visiting poet in eastern Washington, where Young Bear taught in 1987, and a pow-wow in White Swan, Washington., that Pat haunts Edgar's memories.

Edgar Bearchild and Ted choose to reside in the Settlement, attempting to know, to connect with their heritage, their elders, their Star-Medicine religion. In such a localized world, small happenings loom large as adventures, as all-important moments of living. Edgar says it best in his memories of Ugly Man Pat: "Due to our geographic and cultural isolation, we were sentimental. Twenty-four hours after anything occurred, it was recollected."

One of the largest loomings and most magically real narratives is "The Supernatural Strobe Light," an at once ancient and futuristic encounter by Edgar and his post-1973 girlfriend/wife, Selene Buffalo Husband, with three evil, defiant owls.

Edgar wanders West to Claremont, California, as Young Bear himself did when he attended Pomona College in 1970, and Ted Facepaint visits him. Together they experience an "eclectic California" of sex, drugs, and rock'n'roll. Edgar's struggling years as a young poet—his applications for various grants such as a creative-writing fellowship from the Maecenas Foundation, his years holed up, waiting for inspiration on the Settlement, virtually papered with paper, pasted to his body like a cocoon and hanging, suspended, awaiting some kind of metamorphosis of genius—now fully and finally come to fruition.

Look! He has come through! Young Bear has arrived! We too can chant with Pat "Dirty" Red Hat, in the words of his shared song, "Shining Black Eagle Child Dancer":

"Come and look at the best dancer; come and look at this Black Eagle Child, the one who shines so."[22]

PART
THREE

CHICANO VISTAS

INTRODUCTION

The view provided by Chicano/a literature is large and expansive, a *vista grande*. It is more than just one panel in the panorama of the literature of the American West and more encompassing than literature *about* the Mexican American or about Mexican-American experiences in the United States.

Although nationalistic in its impulse, Chicano literature draws from and reinforces all of Hispanic literature, Latino literature, and, indeed, world literature. For Chicano vistas are the vistas not just of the U.S. and Mexico, but of North and South America and of all Spanish-speaking cultures, their settlement and their diaspora, literatures written in Spanish and English and indigenous and mestizo literatures.

Readers who categorize Chicano/a literature as politics or propaganda, or who dismiss it as Southwest or California regionalism fail to realize how truly encompassing Chicanismo is as it expands into the next century beyond the Chicano civil and land rights movements of the 1960s.

Chicano/a literature, however, and the spirit of "la raza," "la gente," "el pueblo," and "carnalismo" bespeak an impulse, a force that promises not only to reclaim but to dominate American if not world literature. It is the primal force of empowerment of indigenous peoples, and Chicano/a literature claims *la tierra* as home to those peoples. Hence it gains power not just from struggle but from the call for harmony with one's homeland and with the earth. Along with American Indian literature, its close kin, Chicano/a literature is the literature that champions the environment, champions "ecology" and the restoration of mythic intuition and indigenous understanding.

The Chicano/a canon is, naturally enough, expanding. In the essays that follow I focus on two of the fathers of Chicano literature, Rudolfo A. Anaya and Jimmy Santiago Baca, both of whom live in Albuquerque, New Mexico.

They have influenced each other's work. They have influenced all other Chicano/a writers. And Anaya and Baca have joined the canon of not just American but world literature. Baca and Anaya are Chicano writers, New Mexico writers, United States writers, transcontinental writers— great writers judged by any standard, regional, national, or aesthetic.

Albuquerque, its stories and its histories, functions as both a replicated and a rediscovered Aztlán for both writers. It is their home, their center, their inspiration. And they draw from this well-spring of creativity with all the fervor of the possessed. They write with what García Lorca calls "el duende." That demiurge of zealous dedication to art and its functions catapults them into the transcendent plane of poets and of prophets. Their obsession with beauty and truth, like that of Welch and Young Bear, brings credence to the visions of their protagonists, the curanderas and shamans who as seers bring others enlightenment. Their own vision and the vistas they open for their readers have made Baca and Anaya revered and acknowledged legislators, as Shelley would say, of their world and ours.

LA LLORONA, MAGIC REALISM,
AND THE FRONTIER

One of the most fascinating female archetypes in contemporary Mexican-American literature is La Llorona, the wailing woman of Hispanic folklore and legend. The figure of La Llorona, in one guise or another, appears in many works of Chicano literature—most notably in Ray John de Aragón's *The Legend of La Llorona*, the *cuentos* of Sabine R. Ulibarrí, and Orlando Romero's *Nambé—Year One*. Nowhere is she more fully realized than in the novels and short stories of Rudolfo A. Anaya. Although Anaya's characterization of La Llorona is varied and complex, the successful adaptation of the legend into fictional character may be understood in relation to magic realism—that paradoxical literary mode which is associated most closely with certain contemporary Latin American writers like Gabriel García Márquez, Jorge Luis Borges, Julio Cortázar, and Carlos Fuentes. Magic realism in fiction, however, by one name or another, runs all the way back to Cervantes' *Don Quixote* and extends as a subspecies of romanticism through centuries of diverse national bodies of literature to the writings of classic United States authors such as Hawthorne, Melville, Poe, Whitman, and Faulkner, and on into postmodern times. To be sure, magic realism plays a major role in contemporary Chicano fiction.

An inquiry into the uses of the La Llorona legend in the fiction of contemporary Mexican-American writers can aid our understanding of several things: the cultural, political, and social assumptions surrounding the portrayal of women in contemporary Chicano fiction; the shifting and elusive definition of magic realism as a literary style and technique; the degree to which contemporary Chicano literature is an integral part of the literatures of the United States and Latin America; and finally, the interdependency of the archetypal evil/good woman with concepts of the frontier generally and the American frontier specifically, albeit localized in rural northern New Mexico.

The kinship between magic realism and literary renderings of women on the frontier is especially intriguing to consider. Because magic realism is such an apparently contradictory term, hard and fast definitions of it—as with the term frontier—are elusive. Art critic Franz Roh is said to have coined the term *magic realism* in the 1920s in response to post-expressionist painting, calling it "a movement that sought to capture the beyond-rational, inner meaning of immediate, exterior reality." And Arturo Uslar Pietri, transferring it to Venezuelan fiction, "used the term to describe the poetic mysteries of human behavior amidst realistic settings."[1] Thought by some to flourish "wherever a veneer of European civilization is imperfectly blended with hidden layers of primitive cultures,"[2] magic realism is rarely linked explicitly to the concept of the frontier. This is surprising in that the confrontation between European civilization and exoticism, primitivism, or alleged savagery, or between "realism" and "magic," is often implicit in definitions of *frontier*, particularly in North and South America.

"Frontier," often synonymous with "West" in the context of the American frontier, is seen both as "the cutting edge for happy American progress" and as a "neutral territory, or middle condition";[3] "the meeting ground of various savagery, and thus . . . a narrow zone of intense ambiguity."[4] It is precisely this kind of ambiguity, the meeting ground of reality and magic, that serves as the basis for magic realism. Recall the necessity for ambiguity in the romance as Hawthorne theorized about it in his preface to The House of the Seven Gables, and practiced in his novels and short stories wherein he "mellowed the lights" and "deepened the shadows."

Using Frederick Jackson Turner's frontier thesis as a point of departure, Edwin Fussell insists that both European and American meanings of the word *frontier*, as political boundary and as edge of settlement, are fused into one frontier metaphor:

> What the American frontier means is [the metaphor's] genesis: a new situation, vaguely sensed, and requiring designation, was denoted by an old word with an adaptable meaning. The mingling of meanings helps explain why the American frontier was sometimes a line and sometimes a space. . . . Either way, the frontier was a figure of speech, gradually but never entirely sloughing European implications as it assumed new functions in a new context. . . . The frontier was the imaginary line between American civilization and nature, or the uncreated future, and everything that came to depend upon that line was ironically reversible.[5]

If one defines magic realism as a literary movement "whose purpose is to penetrate objective reality and reveal the mysterious and poetic qualities underlying the daily lives of a community or a people,"[6] the ambiguities that inform such a movement can also be found in "the periphery" and "the transitional middle" of the frontier.[7]

La Llorona as legend and in its structural and thematic applications in fiction is similarly predicated on cultural, aesthetic, and moral ambiguities. It is because of such blurring of boundaries that magic realism becomes such an appropriate literary vehicle for the legend. The wailing woman's ambiguous real/unreal, historical/fictive presence and her ambivalent treatment by authors (and by narrators and characters) as both attractive and repulsive, beautiful and grotesque, young and old, is due to the fundamental dialectic between the forces of good and the forces of evil; between the archetypal good woman and bad woman which so often in Chicano literature manifest themselves as the woman as virgin, the woman as whore; the woman as saint or mother or sister or wife or daughter, and the woman as *femme fatale*—as seductress; the woman as angel and devil, light and dark, refined and civilized, primitive and "savage."[8]

Such a dialectic is not restricted to any one female of legend or to any national literature or literary genre. Versions of La Llorona (and her ostensibly villainous male counterparts) can be found throughout the fictions of the past and present, including contemporary soap operas which critics of popular culture attempt to explain by means of, among other things, the abundance of appealing "evil" women. One such critic, Marilynn Preston, poses the question this way:

> Why are Evil Women featured at all nowadays? . . .
> Is TV reflecting women the way they are, or the way
> women watching at home wish they could be?
>   Or is something else going on in the culture, something deeper, something darker, something that has to
> do with the male's continual need to punish females
> who want power by portraying them as wicked, ruthless, burnable at the stake?[9]

The prevalence of evil women in contemporary popular culture suggests that the incorporation of the La Llorona legend in contemporary Chicano literature is a reflection of a universal female archetype which merits further analysis. Her ambivalent bad/good identity and her portrayal as sinner and martyred "saint," especially in the seemingly contradictory worlds of the frontier and magic realism, suggest that good and evil seldom exist in pure, undiluted states.

Traditionally in Mexican-American culture the legend of La Llorona is used as a kind of behavioral throttle. Analogous to the bogeyman, La Llorona is a threat to wayward or mischievous children who might stray into certain off-limits or taboo places. "Beware of La Llorona, she is waiting for you," is the typical warning. As in the Anglo-American folksong, "Long Black Veil," wherein a woman walks the hills in a veil, crying and visiting the grave of the dead and ghostly speaker/lover of the lyrics, La Llorona is said to haunt arroyos, rivers, and ditches, forbidden and remote waterways where an unthinking child, usually a boy, might wander or be lured. She does not haunt these god-forsaken "frontiers" simply because of adultery, as in the "Black Veil" folksong (although that is a lesser motif in the legend). Instead, she walks the earth in a perpetual quest (something in the nightmarish Dickensian manner of Marley's ghost or Hawthorne's Ethan Brand or his own veiled minister), searching for her children and weeping not just for their loss but for her own guilt—her crime of murdering her children, slaughtering them, and discarding their bodies. Her appearance, paradoxically, is usually associated with the color white more than with black.

Some versions have her mutilating her children and tossing their bodies in a river or ditch. In any event, she is doomed to wander the earth throughout eternity in search of her dead and lost offspring, and peace of mind—some sort of forgiveness. She seeks other children as replacements that will enable her, so the legend often suggests, to repeat her grisly act. It is in many ways both a strange and a familiar legend, for La Llorona is not the sole property of Hispanic cultures. Medea in Greek mythology and even Isis in Egyptian lore are recognizable "sisters."

La Llorona is fundamentally part of the oral folk tradition, but the most extensive written account is that of Ray John de Aragón who, in a macabre narrative (complete with overly zealous priests, the gothicism of the Spanish Inquisition, and the mob hysteria of witchcraft trials and burnings) tells the story of a La Llorona as a pseudohistorical personage, one Luisa Gertrudis de Panuela, who in late sixteenth-century colonial Mexico loved not wisely but too well.[10] In de Aragón's reenactment, circumstances and motives tend to exonerate La Llorona. She does murder her two children quite gruesomely with a knife. But she is forced to do it as a result of the mental anguish caused by her lover, Juan de Velasco, an aristocrat and son of the then-presumed viceroy of Mexico, Luis de Velasco.

Juan loves Luisa and fathers two children by her; however, he is prevented from marrying her by his parents because she is not of the aristocracy. Rather than give up her two children to Juan and his more acceptable fiancée, María Dolores de Mendoza, and be banished north to New Mexico, she kills her children in a demented frenzy. Due largely to the face-saving scheming of the heartless Luis de Velasco and his wife, and to Juan's belated and ineffective protests (and eventual acquiescence), Luisa is tried as a witch. She is stripped naked and examined for the devil's mark; when a birthmark is found, she is convicted and burned at the stake. Because her children's bodies are stolen from their caskets, and because of her own anguish and guilt, she screams out of the flames for her children, pleading that they be returned to her. Because her sobbing does not cease, the mob shouts, "La mujer llorona no para (the crying woman does not stop)" (p. 83). The mob is incapable of hearing anything but her crying and soon calls her "La Llorona"—the wailing woman. The final twist of the story is one of vengeance. As the mob runs frantically to escape the cries of Luisa, the fire follows them and destroys the viceroy's palace and all of the Velasco and Mendoza families within it. A servant who escapes swears that the spirit of the witch La Llorona has returned to take her revenge and that she will continue to do so. The name of La Llorona becomes associated with fear and loathing in everyone's, especially her accusers', hearts and psyches.

There is more to de Aragón's version of the legend. He frames Luisa's story with an interpolated tale of a fearless young man by the name of Ricardo Valdez. Many years later and far to the north, in Santa Fe, New Mexico, while riding home late at night, Valdez experiences a frightful thing. He sees a fireball and then an aged woman with a "translucent body" which "seemed to float in the night air" (p. 15). He seeks out a nearby dwelling only to be greeted by the woman and the diabolical odor of burnt ashes. It is a scene which, potentially formulaic, is found in varied and ingenious ways throughout the fiction of Ulibarrí, Romero, Anaya, and Ray John de Aragón. Here is de Aragón's description:

> The woman appeared with a hideous, mocking laugh.
> But then her distorted face cracked with lines of sor-
> row. Her pain filled [sic] eyes stressed her inner anguish
> and her inflamed body became a vision of agony while
> the fires of hell burnt around her. She reached out to
> him in a pleading way as if begging for him to help her.
> (p. 17)

Ricardo is an ordinary man in quite clearly fantastic circumstances. Only after being mysteriously transported back to his own home and hearing the explanation of the village curandera, Tía Elena, does Ricardo realize that he met La Llorona face to face. Now under the threat of being singled out by evil forces, Ricardo is instructed by the curandera that he must do something to save his soul. If he does nothing, he is lost to the desires of La Llorona. Whether his experience is natural or supernatural, a nightmare or reality, he must somehow help La Llorona find peace so that she will release him. He speculates that perhaps some written, historical record of La Llorona could exist which, if found, might reveal some clue to his salvation. He sets forth on a quest that uncovers the account of Luisa Gertrudis de Panuela. With the aid of the Franciscan priest Fray Carlos Delgado of San Miguel church, his search takes him to the bat-infested, decayed ruin of the San Gerónimo church where, protected by a statue of the angel of death, he discovers the diary of Luisa's duenna, Josefa, transcribed as a confessional and related by the priest who gave her absolution.

The novel's elaborate interpolation and frame narrative demonstrate just how ominous and obsessive the legend of La Llorona is, even for the reader. Ricardo is symbolically cut by the statue's scythe, which protects the diary, and triggers the disclosure of the aged coffer which holds the diary. The scythe soon disappears. Just as mysteriously, the church is engulfed in flames when Ricardo finishes reading the diary; but he is rescued by Fray Alonso, who tells the "lucky" Ricardo that an old woman was seen in his company but was lost to the fire. Was she real or illusory? Had La Llorona caught up with both her story and Ricardo? The ambiguity follows Ricardo back to Santa Fe. He has still not found the clue to either his salvation from La Llorona's hounding, or for her own peace. What he does find in his own bed, on the first night of his return, is the lost scythe, now bloody.

De Aragón's written account of the legend is obviously not without its magic realism, the kind of ambiguities utilized to such masterful effect by Hawthorne in *The Scarlet Letter* and in stories like "Young Goodman Brown," where women are dramatized enigmatically as "evil" but "good," caught up in a magically real world of witchcraft and Christianity. But de Aragón's comprehensive narration of the La Llorona legend also illustrates some of the reasons for the ambivalences with which the Wailing Woman is regarded. By injecting a conflict between heartless aristocrats and victims driven to evil, he shows why any account of La Llorna must be at once empathic and condemnatory. It illustrates, as well, the isolation and anxiety of the frontier of New Mexico—a place like Hawthorne's New England forest where civilization merges with "savagery," where good confronts evil in actual and allegorical terms.

Another New Mexico writer who adapts the La Llorona legend into his fiction is Sabine R. Ulibarrí. In his two volumes of *cuentos*, *Tierra Amarilla* and *Mi Abuela Fumaba Puros*, La Llorona makes more than one important appearance. Aside from his serious and frightening story of the double, "Hombre sin Nombre," he combines northern New Mex-

ico folk humor with magic realism in a unique voice and style. His dramatizations of La Llorona take on, for the most part, a humorous—certainly
a humane—slant.[11]

In "Brujerías o Tonterías?" (Witcheries or Tomfooleries?") Ulibarrí
poignantly connects the La Llorona legend to the idea of "una herencia,
una intrahistoria" (a heritage, an intrahistory) of the narrator/persona
who as a small boy encounters a beautiful but frightening woman one night,
a woman he knows is La Llorona herself until he discovers it is only a
woman named Atanacia, the retarded wife of a neighbor, Casiano. Her
convincing plan is to assume the disguise of La Llorona and roam the
darkness seeking to frighten her unfaithful husband out of his philander-
ing. Ulibarrí's narrator—a speaker at least partially autobiographical—is
disappointed that it is Atanacia and not La Llorona whom he meets—a
characteristically ambivalent response. Again, typically, the occasion for
this meeting is remote, the "frontier" of Tierra Amarilla in rural, northern New Mexico. The experience is associated with a kind of atavism
reaching back to a biological "frontier"—to earlier, more primitive times
and places; a dark night lit brightly by the moon; the vestigial times and
places of the subconscious. The wail of Atanacia/La Llorona is identified
in its seductiveness with "un atavismo vital, onírico [oneiric] y singular."[12]
The love and the fear in Ulibarrí's portrayal of La Llorona are deeply
felt—an ambivalent attraction and repulsion of woman typical of such
high romantic works as Coleridge's "Christabel" and Keats's "La Belle
Dame sans Merci."

In his exotically beautiful novel/autobiography, *Nambé—Year One*,
Orlando Romero pays another homage to the female principle, "La hembra," in a number of forms. Portrayed as a legendary Gypsy (a Flora or
earth-mother figure) who, with enchanting green eyes and a dancing bear,
in turn captivated the great grandfather, the grandfather, and then the father of the book's poet/protagonist, Mateo Romero, she now haunts Mateo
as a memory—a spirit and an incarnation of *hembrisma*, the female principle. Here again the techniques and assumptions of magic realism por-
tray La Llorona—like the Gypsy—as an idea and as a woman. The exoticism of the Gypsy, her actions and her environment, carries over into
Mateo's meeting with La Llorona. The same kind of "oneiric atavism,"
"intra history," or blood consciousness that Ulibarrí speaks about in his
Tierra Amarilla encounter with La Llorona is present in Mateo's ambivalent love for and fear of the Gypsy in all her guises. Mateo Romero is
even more effusive in his attraction to womanhood.

As with de Aragón and Ulibarrí, the "frontier" of northern New Mexico is the setting for Mateo's meeting with La Llorona. This time, however it is not Santa Fe or Tierra Amarilla. It is Nambé, an even older set-

tlement in what is known as, appropriately in connection with magic realism, "the land of enchantment." Now both a village and a pueblo ruin (another kind of "frontier," or threshold), Nambé was in the beginning a pueblo of Tewa-speaking peoples. The name *Nambe* is said to mean "people of the roundish earth," and Mateo is conscious throughout the book of the heritage (in Ulibarri's term, the "intrahistory") represented in the actual human bones upon which the pueblo ruins stand.[13] In Romero's adaptation of the La Llorona legend, Mateo remembers meeting an old hag (known locally as "La Bartola," the bearded or wattled woman), when, as a young boy, he was going fishing. An outcast, always taunted by youths who throw eggs at her dilapidated house, she roams the environs between Nambé pueblo and Nambe village with her pack of wild dogs. The dogs charge Mateo and, frightened, he describes the old woman as she surprisingly rushes to calm them:

> Her hair was wild and straight, between silver gray and sun bleached [*sic*] white. It was like the colorless cadavers and animal skulls that seem lost to the ties of living, which in reality have been blessed [*sic*] to white by natural sterilization. She wasn't ugly, but her stature and physical appearance was [*sic*] beyond comprehension. . . .
>
> It looked like she was wearing a misshapen gunny sack with old wrinkled boots protruding from within and beneath the hem. The top that covered the strange dress looked like an old fashioned [*sic*] leather vest. It was a faded purple as if irises had died on it.
>
> Her skin was brown like her adobe house and just as cracked. Her hands were thorny and calloused. Yet in all this chaos, shouting and barking, there was such a strange aura of peace coming from her wild green eyes that I wasn't sure if my life had been threatened at all by the pack of wild dogs.[14]

The well-meaning old woman scolds her dogs and comforts the boy. As suggested in the ambivalent imagery used in describing her dress ("a faded purple as if irises had died on it"), the boy senses beauty in the *vieja*'s unsightliness, and feels a human, mothering spirit when she hugs him:

> Unexpectedly she pulled me towards her and put my head between her sagging breasts. I smelled the sweat of the earth and felt the coarseness of her dress and in

my closeness I felt the gentle flutter of her beating
heart. It was soft and sweet, like the cooing of doves.
(p. 62)

Such an intuitive message of love and caring is ironically foregrounded against the legend of La Llorona who, as a wailing killer, searches constantly to snare an unsuspecting child. Mateo is invited into the old woman's house. She offers the hospitality not of gingerbread and candy like the witch in "Hansel and Gretel" but of delicious *carne seca* and of stories with a confessional lilt, stories charged with emotion by the loneliness in the old woman's fertile, Gypsy-like green eyes.

It seems that La Bartola's son, Manuelito, was persecuted for being the son of a wandering Turko, a gypsy, and for having a mother who had defied convention in her love for the gypsy. Manuelito and his mother received even more harassment from the local villagers when he survived a terrible plague that killed most of the other children in surrounding villages. (This parallels the way that La Llorona suffers at the hands of the hysterical mob crying for death at the stake in de Aragón's narrative.) The next spring, when Manuelito tended his flock of goats in the mountains, he disappeared. His mother conjectures that he was stolen and sold. For years she "wandered up and down the canyons of Tres Ritos wailing"; but she never found her child (p. 64). La Bartola's hospitality to Mateo is but a pitiful substitute for a reunion that never takes place.

Romero's tender descriptions of this interlude between an old ostracized woman and a frightened boy are as touching as any rendering of the deep reverence for motherhood and sympathy for victims that characterize Chicano literature. Romero's love of women more generally, although tinged with some small ambivalence, represents one of the most absolute tributes to femininity and "La hembra" to be found. Such treatment is, however, consistent with the ancient outlines of the legend of La Llorona.

The most aesthetically satisfying portrayal of La Llorona in contemporary Chicano fiction is found in the novels and short stories of Rudolfo A. Anaya, who masterfully realizes the full potential of magic realism inherent in the legend. La Llorona is adapted in many ways—literally and metaphorically—through all of Anaya's works, including his trilogy, *Bless Me, Ultima* (1972); *Heart of Aztlán* (1976); and *Tortuga* (1979)—as well as in his collection of short stories, *The Silence of the Llano* (1982); and in his short novel, *The Legend of La Llorona* (1984), which serves as a kind of culmination to Anaya's fascination with the myth of the wailing woman. She appears in more oblique, subtle, but still thematic ways in Anaya's novel *Alburquerque* (1992).[15]

La Llorona is by no means the sole portrayal of a woman—either as stereotype, archetype, or outright character—in Anaya's fiction. But one senses that because the legend is so encompassing in what it says about woman as lover, as wife, as mother, and as outcast, some aspect of La Llorona is present in greater and lesser degrees in most of Anaya's images of women as both major and minor characters. Certainly the three "witches," the diabolical Trementina (turpentine) sisters in *Bless Me, Ultima*, appear as magical manifestations of La Llorona whose presence as an idea, as legend haunts the young protagonist, Antonio Márez. She is everywhere along the river between the novel's two remote villages of Guadalupe and Las Pasturas—pursuing Tony as surely as the Trementina sisters and their devil father, Tenorio, and his black horse, Diablo, pursue the curandera and protectress of the story, Ultima, as she tries to guard herself and Antonio with every possible means—especially with her owl, the embodiment of her very soul.

Antonio's mother, María Luna Márez, is more representative of the Virgin of Guadalupe than of La Llorona. However, the sequential losses of her three older sons—the first to the war and the second to the city; and then her loss of Antonio to experience and adulthood in the course of the novel—suggest and are reinforced by trauma of La Llorona's loss of her two sons. To some extent, hers represents the loss of children experienced by all mothers.

Ultima is the androgynous reconciliation and synthesis of La Llorona and the Virgin of Guadalupe. She is dedicated to the forces of good, but not beyond suspicion as a witch, albeit a good one. When put to the test in one of the novel's key confrontational scenes, she passes through the doorway marked with special needles meant to ward off witches. But she does so only because the distraction of her owl's flight to gouge out one of Trementina's eyes allows the needles ambiguously either to fall or be taken down. The mob of crazed men who follow Tenorio is again adapted from the La Llorona legend. Ultima, too, in an act associated with La Llorona's murders, does not kill her own children like the wailing woman of legend; rather, she murders two of the Trementina sisters, not with a knife, but by sticking needles in dolls constructed out of mud in their likeness.[16] In these ways, Anaya works out his new variations on an old motif in his first novel, *Bless Me, Ultima*.

In Anaya's second novel, *Heart of Aztlán*, La Llorona is heard in the wailing of the sirens of the police cars that chase the young pachucos and "squadros" who live in the barrio of Barelas and wage large and small battles with socioeconomic injustices. The wailing of La Llorona thus metaphorically provides the background music, the sound track for the gang fights and rumbles between the gringo stompers and the pachucos and *vatos*, between the reign of marijuana and of common sense, between the wealthy country-club set and the residents of Barelas, between the Santa Fe railroad and its workers. But for Clemente Chávez, the adult protagonist of the novel, the encounter takes on a less metaphorical and more mythical outline. For it is Clemente, under the tutelage of the blind seer, Crispín, who visits the witch of "la piedra mala" and enters a magical journey of self-discovery that takes him into the evil rock where he is immersed in underground waters outside of time. Inside the rock he is transported to an imaginary mountain but also to a real epiphany which directs him to the very heart of Aztlán, the fabled homeland of his people. Thanks to the magic pins which Crispín gives Clemente as an offering to the rock, it is receptive to his request. Thus he rises from despair to become the political and spiritual leader and prophet of his people. And all because he dares to meet the bruja by the water, agrees to meet the keeper of the magical black rock—a woman who although flesh and blood is also a manifestation of La Llorona.

In the witch of *la piedra mala* Anaya combines the legendary La Llorona with the archetypal story of Faust. For in his quest to know the true whereabouts of Aztlán, the magical yet real homeland of his people, Clemente is tempted to bargain away his own soul, to become the pawn of the old woman and her devotion to the evil rock.

In a lonely hut by the irrigation ditch that runs parallel to the river, the witch of *la piedra mala* stands guard over the rock. She is, in La Llorona terms, its mother. Not only does she reside perpetually by the waters of the ditch and the river, but the wailing associated with La Llorona is echoed in her incantation and in the music of the rock. Note the magic realism in Clemente's entry into the rock, told with a kind of psychedelic, cinematic effect out of Hawthorne via Disney:

> She turned to Clemente and made him sit facing the rock, and she instructed him carefully. First he was to place the silver pins and needles on the rock, and when he did it seemed to writhe with life. The pins disappeared slowly. Clemente felt his stomach heave and he turned to find Crispín, but the old woman hissed a sharp command: "Look at the rock! It is death to look anywhere except at the rock! Look only at the fire in the rock . . . You will enter the rock . . . You will find the door in a grain of sand . . . you will find the door to the mountain . . . you will find the seven wombs of the earth. . . ." She began to chant and the room began to spin slowly around the rock.
>
> The journey began. Clemente was aware of the

preparations. He saw Crispín get ready and he repeated
the motions of the old man. The shining rock became
a door which they could enter. At the entrance the old
woman greeted them. She gave Clemente a bitter potion to drink: it fell like bile into his empty stomach
and a numbing sensation spread throughout his body,
quieting the swirling vertigo. She pointed and again he
looked at the rock and this time a melody drew him
into the river in which the rock tumbled.[17]

The witch of *la piedra mala* is simultaneously evil and the answer to
Clemente's alienation and despair. Because she ushers him into the paradoxes of a universe in a grain of sand, a mountain in a rock, he becomes
a prophet for his people and leads them through nonviolent protest to
throw off the oppressive yoke of the union bosses and the railroad where
most of the residents of Barelas work. Surely the shop whistle, also metaphorically associated with the wailing of La Llorona, contributes to the
mood of magic realism; but it is the old bruja who most dramatically and
importantly serves as the focus for magic realism and the legend of La
Llorona.

Anaya's use of La Llorona is at first glance less prominent in *Tortuga*
and in the stories of *The Silence of the Llano*. She is, however, present in
both instances and she resurfaces fully in his novella, *The Legend of La
Llorona*. In *Tortuga*, La Llorona provides the allusive basis for the characterization of Ismelda and Josepha, the two ordinary but magical hospital aides and inspirational "healers" in the novel. La Llorona is also
suggested in the neglected patient, the freakish, dwarflike cripple, Cynthia. All three of these characters are accepted and loved by the temporarily paralyzed protagonist of the story, Tortuga.

Ismelda first appears dressed in white, occupied with work, ostensibly
as a nurse's aide, doing beds, sweeping floors, but actually concerned
with lifting the spirits of Tortuga and initiating him into the legend of the
restorative mineral waters of the mountain (also called Tortuga) located
just outside the hospital in the town of Agua Bendita. Both Ismelda and
her friend Josepha are cast in the role of mothering the patients in the
hospital for crippled children. Tortuga is obsessed with Ismelda, haunted
by her, and they soon fall in love. She is described as dark-featured with
eyes that "flashed with the fire of life."[18] She is the daughter of a wandering gypsy with green eyes, from whom she inherits her eyes, the green
eyes that Tortuga sees in his dreams. An obvious earth mother, like
Romero's Gypsy, she enables Tortuga, with the help of the skilled and humane doctor, Steel, to walk out of the hospital the following spring. (An-

other of her allies is the all-knowing Solomon, who, although in an iron lung, gains his omniscience and omnipresence through special telepathic powers.) Josepha, even more earthy than Ismelda, jokes with Tortuga about his potency and virility as a male, and tells stories "about the people and the land" (p. 57). In reality Ismelda and Josepha are both simple hospital orderlies who live by the river and come to work at the hospital; but magically, they are possessors of the healing powers of the curandera.

In his night dreams Tortuga sees La Llorona, and when he awakens a strange presence lingers in his room; he imagines the presence of La Llorona combined with the identity of Ismelda. Tortuga tells of his fright and love:

> In the hallway all is quiet, but here in the room a
> strange presence breathes. My hair tingles, for a mo-
> ment I believe that la Llorona has followed me out of
> the dream and into my room.
>
> Who's there, I whisper in the darkness. . . . and I
> think of Ismelda, is she safe, sleeping in her house by
> the river, does the wailing woman visit her dreams or
> is it we who are men the only ones tormented by the
> witch? Who visits Ismelda's dreams? . . .
>
> Who's there, I call again . . . and wonder if Ismelda
> is sister to la Llorona . . . daughter of the same womb . . .
> companion to those young girls which shared the altar
> with me the last day of my childhood and who return
> to haunt every dream which seeks to tell me that in my
> innocence lies the answer to the question I seek now.
> Why me? Who was I then? Who am I now?" (p. 67)

The complexity of the La Llorona myth in terms of gender roles, of male/female relationships, and of the male psyche, and the art that can make one myth all-inclusive, encompassing good and evil women, young and old, past and present, idea and actuality—all of this is dramatized in Tortuga's linking La Llorona with Ismelda and with the girls of his first holy communion. In Tortuga's nightmare La Llorona haunts him with just such puzzles:

> You are the son I butchered for love, she cries, you are
> the son I lost at war, the babe forced into my womb by
> the power of your father, abandoned child. She reaches
> out and her long fingernails cut through my flesh as I
> struggle and cry for help in the smoldering darkness of

the ash heap. Do not fear me, she cries, I am your
mother, your sister, your beloved . . . I suckled you at
my breasts, sang lullabies for you, wrapped you in rags
torn from my skirts . . . I am all the women you have
violated. . . .(p. 66)

Similarly, the paradox of finding beauty and something to love in the
ugliness of Cynthia dramatizes Tortuga's realization that only in the all-
encompassing love of all women is the future ensured and the life force
affirmed. When the entire ward heads off to town and a movie in a day
of carefree frolic (reminiscent of the fishing trip McMurphy organizes in
Ken Kesey's *One Flew over the Cuckoo's Nest*), Anaya dramatizes this
sense of love for all humanity through the magic realism of that familiar
theater pastime, making love. First horrified by Cynthia's gray and aged
face in the early weeks of his hospital stay, Tortuga, on the mend, finds
Cynthia "beautiful" enough to make love to. The message: through suffering comes love, and while watching, appropriately enough, a Franken-
stein movie, wherein the monster is cheered as heroic by the crippled and
deformed children, Tortuga reaches out, in essence, for the witch of La
Llorona in Cynthia and for the innocent first holy communion girls—
together intertwined somehow with Ismelda, with *hembrisma* and the female principle in dwarfish Cynthia:

"Kiss me," Cynthia begged, clinging to me, crawling
up my lap to press her twisted face against mine. "I've
never been kissed before—"
I looked into her eyes and swallowed the scream
at my throat. I reached around her hump and drew her
close to me. Somewhere beyond the clamor which filled
the theatre I heard the rattle of the tambourines . . .
and in the light which flashed across Cynthia's face and
in her eyes which held love for me I suddenly saw the
first communion girls waving at me. . . . (p. 150)

In this scene magic realism brings about the transformation which
takes place in Tortuga's mind. Cynthia, portrayed as sexually repulsive, is
transformed by the power of love into the virginal purity associated with
the communion girls. In his mind Tortuga sees Ismelda wave to him in ap-
proval and "beat her tambourine tenderly, softly, bringing out its moaning song" (p. 151). By association, wailing is changed to the "moaning
song" of Ismelda's tambourine. In his final dream, in the springtime, just
before being released to return to his home in the north, Tortuga dreams

that Ismelda leads him and the other patients in his ward to the top of
Tortuga mountain. Crutches are thrown away, and in another magical
moment, at once apocalypse and apotheosis, the mountain floats into the
sky while the earth below it is destroyed and made new again by the
forces of fire and water. Tortuga learns later, when saying goodbye, that
Ismelda shared the same magic dream. It is that dream which serves as
the basis for their future together, for he is determined to return for her.
And she promises to wait:

> "Maybe someday we can make that dream come
> true—" I said, and I told her I loved her and that
> someday I was coming back for her . . . someday when
> I was stronger and I could understand the magic and
> the joy which flowed through me and tortured me so
> much . . . someday when all that we had seen and
> shared would have a meaning. I held her in my arms
> and kissed her warm, dark hair, her eyelids, her throat,
> her face and cheeks which were wet with tears, and she
> held my face in her gentle hands and told me she loved
> me and that she would be waiting for me forever.
> (p. 195).

Ismelda, Josepha, and Cynthia, characterized by Anaya as extensions
of the good/evil woman represented in the legend of La Llorona, guard
the "frontiers" of gender and health. The legend's magic is encompassed
in the magical realism of the novelist.

La Llorona is more obliquely present in *The Silence of the Llano*, especially in the title story and "The Road to Platero," both of which depend for much of their effect on their setting, the Llano Estacado, or
"staked plains," which is so important to the locale of *Bless me, Ultima*
and serves as the point of departure for *Heart of Aztlán*. The power and
significance—what Anaya calls the "magic"—of words, when considered in relation to silence, is another major theme of "The Silence of the
Llano" and "The Road to Platero." Solitude is one of the distinguishing
traits of the frontier known as the *llano*, with its wide-open spaces and
few villages such as Las Animas and Platero. It is the landscape of folk
tales and the oral tradition as well, a tradition which Anaya simulates in
his narrations. It is the land of strange occurrences and of taboos—in
these stories the taboo of incest.

Rafael, the solitary man in "The Silence of the Llano," loses to death
first his parents, then his wife. Her death is brought on by the birth of her
namesake, her daughter Rita. For seven years the girl is raised by the mid-

wife, Rufina, who grows to love her like a mother. But in keeping with the loneliness of the llano, Doña Rufina dies too. For the next nine years Rafael never speaks to his daughter. She hears no human voices and matures into womanhood puzzled but captivated by the changes in her body as well as in her mind and her fantasies. A party of hunters intrudes upon the solitude of Rafael and his daughter, and one day while he is away from the house, one of the men returns and rapes the girl. Rafael runs from the pain and the tragedy of the event, for when he sees his daughter reaching out to him from the bed, he also sees his wife. La Llorona is never mentioned directly but Rafael is not permitted to escape from the double vision of his daughter and wife. He is haunted by the memory of his wife and her death and by the sight of his daughter's violation and her crying out of his name, "Rafael, Rafael."

Thrown from his horse, he is knocked unconscious, and after he awakens he stumbles back to the ranch, where he tries to sleep in a toolshed. But he is bothered by the ghostly presence of his wife/daughter:

> Through the chinks of the weathered boards he could
> see the house and the light which burned at the win-
> dow. The girl was awake. All night he stared at the
> light burning at the window, and in his fever he saw
> her face again, her pleading eyes, the curve of her
> young breasts, her arms as she reached up and called
> his name. Why had she called his name? Why? Was it
> the devil who rode the whirlwind? Was it the devil who
> had come to break the silence of the llano? He groaned
> and shivered as the call of the owl sounded in the night.
> He looked into the darkness and thought he saw the
> figure of the girl walking to the water tank. She bathed
> her shoulders in the cold water, bathed her body in the
> moonlight.[19]

Still tormented at dawn, he sees the figure of the girl/wife on the woodblock, "calling his name, smiling and coaxing him as a demon of hell would entice the sinner into the center of the whirlwind."[20] Tormented by the guilt of the seduction, he grabs an axe and splits the air trying to kill the apparition. But when he looks up he sees the face of the wife/girl at the window. Here the murderous act of La Llorona is reversed and Rafael might be viewed as, in effect, striking back at the women he both fears and loves.

Rafael tries one last time to escape, and mounts his horse to ride into oblivion. But a dark whirlwind rises, and in the center of it he sees a woman. "She did not smile, she did not call his name, her horse was the dark cloud which towered over him, the cracking of her whip a fire which filled the sky."[21] He is directed back to the house, back to the water tank where, watching his daughter bathe, he speaks her name, resolved to meet the future with her, with "Rita," the name that was also his wife's.

"The Silence of the Llano" is a disturbing story, unbelievable on a superficial reading, but true in its dramatization of what silence and loneliness, fear and love can do between a father and daughter.

The legend of La Llorona also helps give form to Anaya's most successful short story, "The Road to Platero." The guilts and torments of the violated taboo of incest again provide the focus of the story. Narrated by a young boy, the story tells of the mutual destruction, the violent double murder of his mother and his father, both of them locked in a love/hate battle of the sexes. The narrator's young and beautiful mother, Carmelita, is haunted by her incestuous involvement with her father—once one of the most handsome men of the llano; a man who rode a splendid red stallion in life and still rides it in death, haunting the road to Platero and the minds and memories of both Carmelita and her husband.

The narrator's father, a vaquero whose jingling and flesh-cutting spurs symbolize his domination over both his horses and his wife, calls the wife "whore" and "witch" and promises that he will control her forever and that his killing of Carmelita's father was well deserved. But he is tormented by the old vaquero's ghost, a signal for Carmelita to plunge a dagger into her husband's chest.

Carmelita, as a kind of La Llorona figure, is mother, wife, and murderer, stabbing her husband to death in this version, rather than her son. But the son carries the memory of what happens that fateful night, for his mother is also killed: her throat is cut by her husband's spurs as they fall arm in arm to the floor where they struggle and die in a fatal embrace. Revenge has had its way and the ghost of the old vaquero, which haunted the road to Platero, is gone.

In *The Legend of La Llorona* Anaya casts the legend in the context of the Spanish conquest of Mexico and the relationship between Cortez and his mistress, Malinche. Long seen by many as a traitor to her people for her cooperation with Cortez, Malinche is portrayed as a prototypical La Llorona figure who both betrays and is betrayed, a woman and a goddess who murders her children in a sacrificial attempt to save Mexico from Spanish tyranny and dominion. Anaya uses ambiguity to great effect, in his portrayal of Malinche as La Llorona, reclaiming both history and the supernatural legacy of the myth.

Anaya's version of the history/story of Malinche/La Llorona begins in 1516 in Mexico-Tenochtitlán as the people experience the end of a fifty-two-year cycle on the Aztec calendar and await the return of the great plumed serpent god, Quetzalcóatl. Cortez and his Spanish soldiers come instead, however, and for a time the captain-general is mistaken for the god. It is because of Malintzin (mispronounced by Cortez as Malinche) that the captain both wins and loses his hold on Mexico City and the new world of Spanish exploration and colonization.

Anaya spends little time with the battles or with Montezuma's captivity and death. Rather, the emphasis is placed on the relationship between Malinche and the captain, who in Anaya's portrayal becomes representative of all conquistadors, if not all men, in his disregard of women's feelings.

It is only with the help of Malinche that the captain is able to gain sway over the people. While he tears down the old Aztec idols and religion in an attempt to break the people's will, Malinche reveres the old ways and honors the old shamans and priests, secretly rearing her twin sons in the ancient religion, and frequenting with them the subterranean temple of the old gods of sacrifice.

When another *femme fatale*, Princess Isabella, comes to Mexico to take Cortez back to the good graces of the Spanish monarchy, a triangle of jealousy and intrigue ensues. Cortez betrays Malinche, Isabella betrays Cortez, and Malinche betrays her sons by offering them up in sacrifice as the first warriors whose blood must be spilled to throw off the ruthless, proselytizing Spanish hegemony.

Malinche retreats with her sons to the sacred lake where the ancients first envisioned the eagle with a snake in its beak high atop a giant nopal and were convinced that it was a sacred site on which to build Tenochtitlán. There she follows the vision of the war gods and with an obsidian knife murders both boys and tosses their bodies into the burning sacred lake. Thence will rise the new warriors to conquer, in turn, their conquerors. In her despair and madness Malinche instills fear in all who see her—the soldiers who come in search for her, and the captain, who knows he shares largely in this horrific crime, a crime against his wife and against his sons. From that time forward their story is present in the haunting cries of a woman wailing for her lost children.

In *The Legend of La Llorona*, devoted solely to an empathetic, historically contextual account of the legend, Anaya advances the notion not just of fear and loathing, or of the pain of motherly sacrifice, but understanding of spiritual belief which transcends the personal and the temporal.

CURANDERISMO AND WITCHERY IN THE
FICTION OF RUDOLFO A. ANAYA

The importance of female figures in the fiction of Rudolfo A. Anaya goes beyond La Llorona. I want to examine a bit further *Bless Me, Ultima* and *Heart of Aztlán*. The character of the aged curandera, Ultima, in her role as godmother and spiritual-physical protectress is of primary concern; however, the network of images of women in Anaya's work goes beyond La Llorona and Ultima to include witchery and the influence of La Virgen de Guadalupe. Only in attempting to understand Anaya's representation of women and maternity in Chicano/a culture can one appreciate the author's role—an extension of his male narrators, Antonio Márez and Jason Chávez, respectively—as poet-hero questing for the magical restorative power of the word, of art, myth, and the creative imagination—here manifested in the novel.

Anaya's novels (especially *Ultima*) can be read as fictional autobiographies affirming Anaya's belief in the poetic rendering of one's ethnic identity and heritage (significantly, Anaya dedicates *Ultima* "Con Honor Para Mis Padres" and *Aztlán* "to the good people of Barelas"). *Ultima* and *Aztlán* dramatize these words of Anaya's about writing:

> Writing is not easy. It is a lonely, and oftentimes unappreciated endeavor. But I had to keep creating, I had to keep trying to organize all the beautiful, chaotic things into some pattern. Writing is never quite learned. I have to rewrite and rewrite each manuscript before I'm satisfied. . . . It's easy. You just have to sit down and write, write, write, and write . . . *hasta que te lleva la madre, y las almorranas*.[1]

It is this theme of literature as heroic, of poet as hero in search of the maternal, creative, protective, and inspirational spirit, that allows Anaya's narratives to transcend gender and ethnicity and to render literature universal. C. G. Jung's thoughts on the anima and animus in *The Relations between Ego and the Unconscious* can help with such a reading of Anaya.

In Jungian terms, Ultima may be seen as an anima figure. Her role as heroine echoes Jung's view that "the whole nature of man presupposes woman, physically and spiritually. His system is tuned in to woman from the start, just as it is prepared for a quite definite world where there is water, light, air, salt, carbohydrates, etc. The form of the world into which he is born is already inborn in him as a virtual image."[2] Ultima and her sought-after blessing represent the destiny of the Márez family (and by extension of La Raza), and particularly of Antonio, the young-old hero-narrator.

In her tutelage of Antonio, Ultima underscores Jung's assertion about woman and the feminine quality of the soul:

> Woman, with her very dissimilar psychology, is and always has been a source of information about things for which a man has no eyes. She can be his inspiration; her intuitive capacity, often superior to man's can give him timely warning, and her feeling, always directed towards the personal, can show him ways which his own less personally accented feeling would never have discovered.[3]

Conversely, Ultima's animus imposes itself on Antonio and his facility with words and the part they play in his destiny. In this context Jung says,

> The animus is the deposit, as it were, of all woman's ancestral experiences of man—and not only that, he is also a creative and procreative being, not in the sense of masculine creativity, but in the sense that he brings forth something we might call the *logos spermatikos*, the spermatic word. Just as a man brings forth his work as a complete creation out of his inner feminine nature, so the inner masculine side of a woman brings forth creative seeds which have the power to fertilize the feminine side of man.[4]

This reading can account for Ultima's ambivalent, androgynous presence in the novel as a mediator between male and female tensions in Antonio's development—his mother and her people, the Lunas of the still valley, the earth, the priesthood, farming, and the procreative forces of the moon; his father and his people, the Márez lineage, the llano, movement, the wind, the sea, wanderlust, and the life of a vaquero. Consistent with her name, Ultima is at once comforting and courageous, surrogate mother and father; she is curandera and bruja; spirit and person, human and animal; mortal and immortal, revered and feared.

Antonio's explanations of the significance of Ultima's arrival at the Márez home early in the novel point to this duality in Ultima's character. Commenting on his father's questioning of Ultima's effect on the children, Antonio says,

> I knew why he expressed concern for me and my sisters. It was because Ultima was a curandera, a woman who knew the herbs and remedies of the ancients, a miracle-worker who could heal the sick. And I had heard that Ultima could lift the curses laid by brujas, that she could exorcise the evil the witches planted in people to make them sick. And because a curandera had this power she was misunderstood and often suspected of practicing witchcraft herself. (p. 4)

As the novel unfolds, Ultima will prove up to these abilities with the aid of her doppelgänger magic owl. She will evoke in Antonio the unconscious knowledge of dreams past and future as well as the conscious knowledge of "la familia," of sin, guilt, revenge, alienation, and death as well as friendship, community, sacrifice, love, beauty, and immortality. She teaches Antonio "that the tragic consequences of life can be overcome by the magical strength that resides in the human heart" (p. 237). She blesses Antonio "in the name of all that is good and strong and beautiful. . . ." And she tells him: "Always have the strength to live. Love life, and if despair enters your heart, look for me in the evenings when the wind is gentle and the owls sing in the hills, I shall be with you—" (p. 247). Such a Homeric blessing is implicit from the beginning when Antonio dreams of his birth and of Ultima's decisive silencing of the quarrels of his male relatives over his destiny:

> *Cease! she cried, and the men were quiet. I pulled this baby into the light of life, so I will bury the afterbirth and the cord that once linked him to eternity. Only I will know his destiny.* (p. 6)

The mystic communion and kinship between Antonio and Ultima is lyrically evident in their first actual meeting after Antonio's birth—a

meeting that in itself suggests his destiny as poet-hero, recipient of Ultima's, her owl's, and nature's harmonious story and song:

> "Antonio," she smiled. She took my hand and I felt
> the power of a whirlwind sweep around me. Her eyes
> swept the surrounding hills and through them I saw for
> the first time the wild beauty of our hills and the magic
> of the green river. My nostrils quivered as I felt the
> song of the mockingbirds and the drone of the grass-
> hoppers mingle with the pulse of the earth. The four
> directions of the llano met in me, and the white sun
> shone on my soul. The granules of sand at my feet and
> the sun and sky above me seemed to dissolve into one
> strange, complete being.
> A cry came to my throat, and I wanted to shout it
> and run in the beauty I had found. (pp. 10–11)

That cry, that shout, that run is *Bless Me, Ultima*, the novel itself.
Complementing the maternal-paternal myth-reality that Ultima as
anima-animus figure represents, the maternal myths of La Llorona and
La Virgen de Guadalupe also affect Antonio's journey toward manhood
and the artistic expression of that journey which is the novel.

Antonio has many anxious moments because of La Llorona and is first
pursued by her early in the novel, along the river at night, as he witnesses
the death of hunted, war-crazed Lupito and hears his cry for blessing
mingling with the protective, comforting song of Ultima's owl. Later in
Antonio's dreams:

> *Along the river the tormented cry of a lonely goddess
> filled the valley. The winding wail made the blood of
> men run cold.*
> *It is la llorona, my brothers cried in fear, the old
> witch who cries along the river banks and seeks the
> blood of boys and men to drink!* (p. 23)

Lupito as lost soul is associated with Antonio's brothers (particularly
Andrew and his involvement with La Llorona-like prostitutes at Rosie's);
with his friend, Florence (whose death by drowning structurally parallels
Lupito's river-death); and also Narciso, who although lost in alcoholism
is blessed by Antonio, infused with Ultima's spirit of goodness, and absolved in his sacrificial death—all of which is to say that Anaya beautifully and symbolically expands the La Llorona myth as vehicle for his

message of "carnalismo" and "la familia." Throughout the novel, Antonio must contend with various facets of La Llorona witchery, most directly in the evil deeds of Tenorio Trementina and his daughters. Ultima's curanderismo battles the black arts of Tenorio in the most dramatic and sustained conflict in the novel, for the evils of life that Antonio must conquer are most fully symbolized by Tenorio, his daughters, and his vicious black horse, Diablo. From the time of her arrival, Ultima counsels Antonio in the ways of healing. Most seriously this begins when Antonio's uncle, Lucas, ventures to the evil spot by the river where "evil fires" dance:

> These fireballs were brujas on their way to their meeting places. There, it was said, they conducted the Black Mass in honor of the devil, and the devil appeared and danced with them.
> Ay, and there were many other forms the witches took. Sometimes they traveled as coyotes or owls! (p. 81)

Lucas sees the fireballs acquire the form of women engaged in blood ritual and the Black Mass. Moving closer, Lucas bravely challenges the women and notices a resemblance to the Trementina sisters, long considered brujas. Attacked fiercely by them, he saves himself with two sticks crudely fashioned like a cross and by the sacred utterance: "Jesus, María, y José." The mother of the Trementina sisters, before her death, was known to make clay dolls and prick them with needles resulting in the sickness and death of many in the valley. And in this tradition of witchery, Lucas is stricken and escapes death only with Ultima's magic remedies, and Antonio's apprentice, empathic, blood-kin help.

Part of the ritual involves Ultima's confrontation of Tenorio and the announcement that the curse was laid by the gathering of Lucas's clipped hair when he visited Tenorio's shop—establishing the central conflict and leading to Tenorio's vow to kill Ultima, the shooting of Ultima's owl, Antonio's near and Ultima's actual death.

Ultima's confrontation of Tenorio is paralleled with Tenorio's accusing Ultima, in turn, of witchcraft after the death of one of his daughters. The reader, along with Antonio, knows that Ultima has herself fashioned three clay dolls in the likeness of the Trementina sisters and that one doll has mysteriously sagged and bent over, grimacing as if in pain. Through nicely controlled dramatic irony, the reader knows that Ultima's trial for witchcraft is really not absolute, because just when Ultima passes through the door marked with holy needles in the sign of Christ (something witches cannot do), her owl swoops down and gouges out Tenorio's eye with the resulting commotion blinding everyone but young Antonio to the fact that the needles have fallen to the floor. Ironically, Ultima's witchery of love continues to kill the remaining Trementina sisters.

Ultima's witchcraft for the sake of goodness and the protection of Antonio is symbolically associated with the divine motherhood of La Virgen de Guadalupe. Antonio says of his searches for plants and roots in the hills with the curandera: "I felt more attached to Ultima than to my own mother. Ultima told me the stories and legends of my ancestors. From her I learned the glory and the tragedy of the history of my people, and I came to understand how that history stirred in my blood" (p. 115). And this early image that expands through the whole novel fuses Ultima with the sacred Mother: "La Virgen de Guadalupe was the patron saint of our town. The town was named after her. In my dream I saw Ultima's owl lift la Virgen on her wide wings and fly her to heaven. Then the owl returned and gathered up all the babes of Limbo and flew them up to the clouds of heaven" (p. 12). Significantly, it is Antonio's mother's religious teachings and her altar and statue of La Virgen and the rosaries prayed to her every night after supper that provide the basis of his dreams of motherly protection and love:

> We all knew the story of how the Virgin had presented
> herself to the little Indian boy in Mexico and about the
> miracles she had wrought. My mother said the Virgin
> was the saint of our land, and although there were
> many other good saints, I loved none as dearly as the
> Virgin. It was hard to say the rosary because you had
> to kneel for as long as the prayers lasted, but I did not
> mind because while my mother prayed I fastened my
> eyes on the statue of the Virgin until I thought that I
> was looking at a real person, the mother of God, the
> last relief of all sinners. (p. 42)

Ultima functions in a surrogate role, as a flesh and blood incarnation of the Virgin, and because of her own miracles of healing and deliverance she is thought to be a saint herself by those she cures, by Antonio's mother, and, of course, by Antonio, whom she blesses in the name of goodness; Ultima "es una mujer que no ha pecado" (p. 96). Until Antonio receives his own scapular at his first holy communion (a major event in the novel), Ultima gives him her own—a scapular which, instead of the usual bit of cloth at the end with a picture of the Virgin, has a flattened pouch of "helpful herbs" (p. 118). Paradoxically, Ultima is both witch and Virgin mother by means of her powers as a curandera.

In *Heart of Aztlán*, Anaya's second and companion novel to *Bless Me,*

Ultima, motherhood is again a dominant theme, La Llorona is present in the form of the old witch by the water, "la bruja de la piedra mala," and even the shop whistle and police sirens work as symbolic extensions of La Llorona's demon wail. According to legend, the old woman's black rock was brought with her from Mexico to her house in Barelas by the drainage ditch and river. Crazy Willie informs Jason and his "cuates," "Some say she's la Llorona—' . . .You sell your soul to the devil and the black rock brings you money, money and women—"[5] As Willie tells it:

> That piedra mala feeds on pins and needles . . .
> They say the old witch lives only to forge the pins
> and needles for her rock. Bultos and ruidos haunt the
> house. . . . The old woman can't sleep. She is cursed—[6]

In such imagery the rock, suggestively, is her child and it is to this embodiment of La Llorona that Jason's father, Clemente, must come as a supplicant for rebirth, reinforcing again the witch's "motherly" role. Accompanied by the blind seer (curandero of song), Crespín, and his silver needles, Clemente learns the legend of the plumed serpent and "las piedras malas del mundo," visits the witch and her rock, and magically journeys back to the visionary source, the "heart," of legendary Aztlán.

What Ultima's owl is to her, Crespín's ancient guitar is to him. Through it comes the soothing music of past ways and protection from "the black magic of the world." Anaya plays up the witchery involved in Clemente's and Crespín's visit; the bruja's voice cackles with laughter as she greets the pilgrims: "A cat bristled and hissed from a dark corner of the dimly lighted room. The stench from the pot brewing at the stove permeated the small room. 'Entren, entren,' the old woman beckoned them in with bony fingers."[7] And the witchery continues in Anaya's description of the bruja's ritual of the rock:

> She turned to Clemente and made him sit facing the
> rock, and she instructed him carefully. First he was to
> place the silver pins and needles on the rock, and when
> he did it seemed to writhe with life. The pins disap-
> peared slowly. Clemente felt his stomach heave and he
> turned to find Crispín, but the old woman hissed a
> sharp command: "Look at the rock! It is death to look
> anywhere except at the rock! Look only at the fire in
> the rock . . . You will enter the rock . . . You will find
> the door in a grain of sand . . . you will find the door
> to the mountain . . . you will find the seven wombs of

the earth . . . She began to chant and the room began
to spin slowly around the rock.[8]

The witch of the rock administers a calming potion to Clemente and
points to the door in the shining rock through which he passes into what
might be called an ethnic epiphany. Because of his encounter with the
witch and the mystical journey to the magic mountain where he discovers the holy heart of the earth, of Aztlán, Clemente regains his position
of respect as husband and father; furthermore, he becomes a leader of the
oppressed people of the barrio. This rebirth and restoration is achieved
in large part through maternal images. Once again, the sense of the
mother as heroine pervades the novel with a witch aiding in the process
of self- and cultural discovery while an earthly mother-wife perseveres in
her faith in her husband.

In *Curanderismo: Mexican-American Folk Psychiatry* (1972), Ari Kiev
offers a penetrating study of the psychological assumptions behind the
topics of curanderismo and witchery, so important in Anaya's fiction
specifically and Chicano culture generally. According to Kiev's analysis,
women are simultaneously respected and feared. Speaking of the thera-
peutic value of curanderismo, Kiev says:

> While women are highly regarded as mothers and
> wives, they are looked upon as potentially unfaithful
> and untrustworthy, which may partly account for the
> fact that they are heavily watched or chaperoned. Even
> women sought after as sexual objects are considered
> potentially dangerous. This threatening aspect of
> women finds institutional expression in the curandero's
> acknowledgment of beliefs about witches and black
> magic. Viewing these beliefs as projections leads one
> to the inference that women are unconsciously feared.
> This makes sense when one considers the traditional
> overprotectiveness of the Mexican mother who infan-
> tilizes her children and who at the same time desires
> to be viewed as devoted and loyal. Such experiences
> clearly lead to much repressed hostility toward mothers
> which cannot be expressed openly, but can be expressed
> indirectly in projections about dangerous witches and
> temptresses.[9]

This is not to say that Anaya's novels confirm such assumptions and
inferences. Quite the contrary. Certainly they are present in his novels, as

they seem to be in the variant myths of La Llorona and La Virgen de Guadalupe. The lesson, however, which Anaya's heroes learn from his heroines and in turn teach to the reader (assuming Anaya's narrators are his analogs) is that life and ethnic wholeness are to be sought after, loved and not feared, that the old machismo mystique needs updating to incorporate the poet as hero, and that the real magic of life is found through the illusion of art based on anima-animus interdependency. In such a reading, Anaya's fiction confirms the words of British aesthetician R. G. Collingwood in *The Principles of Art* (1958): "Art is the community's medicine for the worst disease of mind, the corruption of consciousness."

AMERICA AS AZTLÁN: LANDSCAPE, MYTH, AND ETHNICITY IN RUDOLFO ANAYA'S *HEART OF AZTLÁN* AND *ALBURQUERQUE,* AND JIMMY SANTIAGO BACA'S *MARTÍN AND MEDITATIONS ON THE SOUTH VALLEY*

As the twentieth century draws to a close, the new literary history and the new American Studies have opened up new ways of perceiving and accounting for, of reimagining the American West. Part of this reimagining is due to Chicano authors, critics, and historians who have shown us more clearly than before what we have always known: that United States history does not happen solely on an East/West axis, as Turner suggested. We see that North/South vectors of cultural influence go much beyond Jamestown and Plymouth, beyond the Civil War, past Yankee/Confederate causality. The American West entails North American and South American contexts and, most profoundly, indigenous, native, folk and oral traditions and the inherent, spiritual, and inspirational connection of literature with myth and with landscape.

Among contemporary Chicano authors, Rudolfo A. Anaya, most directly in *Heart of Aztlán* and *Alburquerque,* and Jimmy Santiago Baca, in *Martín and Meditations on the South Valley,* provide enlightening instances of the writer's reliance on myth and landscape for inspiration and motive, for process and subject in their adaptations in fiction and in verse, respectively, of the myth of Aztlán. These authors apply the myth of Aztlán to Chicano life in the contemporary Southwest, the New West of New Mexico, and the state's largest metropolis, the ancient "Duke City" of Albuquerque.

Although not usually seen as such, Anaya and Baca can be considered part of an older "school" of authors dedicated to "writing the land."[1] Issues of nineteenth- and twentieth-century Anglo-American precursors, influences, and traditions aside, Anaya and Baca prove anew that ideas of myth and landscape are as ageless, as ever present as the land itself and our earliest stirring upon it. It is a "tradition" in keeping with a view of history as medicine and health, as restorative and regenerative, held forth most eloquently by Barry Lopez as the literature of hope:

> We have overlooked or deliberately obscured much in
> our past so as not to disturb the vision of our future.
> We have hung a curtain which cuts us off from truths
> that embarrass or confuse us. . . . The historical depth
> of *people* in North America . . . , is deeper, older than
> the U.S., older than the conquistadores.[2]

In their own imaginative writings, in Anaya's fiction and in Baca's poetry, and in their discussions of their writings and their lives as artists, both authors advocate the importance of myth and landscape and of myth *in* landscape. New Mexico and Albuquerque, which make up much of their landscape of mind and of text, are a landscape regarded by them as *la tierra, la tierra del alma, la sagrada tierra*, a sacred place that determines both who they are and what their writing is about. As Baca phrases it, his dedication to land and to *Chicanismo* is deep and inseparable: "Foremost and always until my last breath I'm going to be a Chicano. . . . I'm not Hispanic, I'm not a Latino, I'm not a Mexican-American. . . . *Soy Chicano, hasta los huesotes* . . . down to the bones.[3]

For Baca, his art is tied directly to his concern "that we've been disenfranchised from our culture, from our language, from our political base, from our land."[4] Politically, outside their advocacy of land and *la lucha* (the struggle) in their writing, both Baca and Anaya are active with the Atrisco Land Rights Council in Albuquerque—a group that seeks to preserve the Atrisco Land Grant of forty-nine thousand acres on the West Mesa, between Coors Boulevard and the Rio Puerco.

Anaya explains his attempts at preserving Albuquerque's Atrisco Land Grant this way (and it is an explanation with implications for his rendering of Albuquerque as Aztlán):

> The old land grants of New Mexico, including the
> Atrisco Land Grant, were established for the good of
> the community, for the good of the settlers who would
> work the land. The land did not belong to any particu-
> lar group of individuals. In fact, the land did not "be-
> long" in the way we think of today when we own title
> to a piece of land.
>
> The land belonged to the community, it was cared
> for, it was the mother earth which nurtured us. It pro-
> vided firewood, grass and water for grazing animals.
> Over centuries the people developed a spiritual attach-
> ment to the land. . . . The land has its spiritual value
> because it nourishes us.[5]

Aztlán, as *la sagrada tierra*, the mother, the nourisher, is for the writer also a muse, an inspirer, the means of artistic revelation and epiphany. All of Anaya's protagonists, especially his artist, author, poet/prophet counterparts, partake of the transforming, inspiring power of landscape, whether by means of rivers, plains, or mountains. Anaya has described the psychological cause (what might be regarded as thought and inspiration transmitted through topography) of transformation in his characters and in himself as an "epiphany in landscape":

> The power of the earth is reflected in its landscape.
> And each one of us defines our relationship to the en-
> ergy of place according to our particular world view.
> Energy flows from the earth, and as one learns how to
> receive that energy one also learns how to live off one's
> energy to dissolve the polarity of metaphor and create
> the unity of epiphany.[6]

Albuquerque's Merced de Atrisco (Atrisco Land Grant), is but one geographical portion of Aztlán, that mythical kingdom representative of home to Anaya and to Baca and to La Raza, La Familia. In its largest geographical sense Aztlán is all of the Southwest.

In *Bless Me, Ultima* Anaya's Aztlán centers around the villages near the Pecos River, the llano and the farms of eastern New Mexico, around Anton Chico, Colonias, Puerto de Luna, and Santa Rosa where he spent his childhood. *Tortuga*, Anaya's third novel in what could be considered Anaya's Aztlán trilogy, finds the mythical kingdom moved a bit south, closer to Truth or Consequences (formerly Hot Springs) and the old Carrie Tingley Hospital for Crippled Children. But Tortuga (the metaphorical transformation of Benjie in *Heart of Aztlán* and the mythic representative of both the specific Turtle Mountain outside the hospital, and Turtle Island, this continent as accounted for in Native American myth) must return again (with Crispín's gift of the Blue Guitar and its legacy of mythic melodies of the land), to Albuquerque and his barrio home, the fictionalized Barelas.

For Baca, Santa Fe and parts of Colorado and Arizona figure into the mappings of Martín's (Baca's renamed autobiographical self) orphanhood and later migrations. But for Anaya and Baca, in their renderings of Albuquerque as Aztlán, the barrio of Barelas, the riverside road of La Vega, the West Mesa, and the foothills of the black mesa near the Isleta reservation that work as boundaries of the South Valley figure more prominently.

Clemente Chávez's discovery in *Heart of Aztlán*, like Antonio's in *Ul-*

tima when the ancient curandera first takes his hand, involves a fusion of self with place, of microcosm with macrocosm. For Antonio, "the granules of sand at my feet and the sun and sky above me seemed to dissolve into one strange, complete being."[7] With the guidance of Crispín and the magic of *the* La Llorona figure, *la bruja de la piedra mala*, Clemente discovers the heart of the heart of Aztlán in his very own heart. He too, in his mountain journey, merges with the universe—Albuquerque's Sandia Mountains becoming the cosmos, the individual fusing with the man-swarm, the moment with eternity.

Clemente's epiphany, his apotheosis as an *hombre de carne y hueso* turned mystic savior and transcendent culture hero, is both inside and outside of time. When he returns from the mountain to Albuquerque and the barrio, he is a changed man, Christlike—as dazed and bedazzled as any of Coleridge's ancient voyagers with flashing eyes and floating hair, worthy of incantations of caution to those who have not ventured beyond the pale. And the people, the shops, the barrio, the larger city (Anglo as well as Chicano) change in echo to his march, his proclamation, *"Soy Aztlán!,"* and his resolve in *la lucha: "Adelante! Adelante!"*

Aztlán pervades Anaya's work. His fiction is an Aztlán chronicle, especially if one goes beyond his Aztlán trilogy into *Alburquerque* (1992), and into the sequels to it, such as *Zia Summer* (1995). It is not surprising, then, to find Clemente Chávez alluded to as a legendary and inspirational figure whose memory and legend pervade the barrio of Barelas—and of "Alburquerque."

Much of the plot of *Alburquerque*, is driven by that urge to know and preserve the true past as the growing city faces the struggle and the promise of its multicultural heritage. Tortuga, or Benjie Chávez, makes his reappearance in this novel as Ben Chávez, now recovered from his early hospitalization and living in and writing about Albuquerque. This middle-aged "Burque" bard (easily seen as an analog to Anaya) has a long-suppressed story to tell: the story of his taboo love affair with Cynthia Johnson, and their son. That story, which Ben wants to write, becomes the very novel itself, *Alburquerque*.

The plot strand in *Heart of Aztlán* which found Jason accused of fathering the baby of the country-club *gringa*, Cindy, is continued and enhanced in *Alburquerque*. Benjie, not his brother Jason, is the real father. And now, all these years later, the child, grown up to become a champion Golden Gloves boxer, Abrán Gonzales, is at first abashed to learn that Sara Gonzales is not his real mother—rather, he is the son of the wealthy but lonely Santa Fe painter, Cynthia Johnson. Abrán's real fight is to learn the identity of his father and, in so doing, to learn his own true identity.

He is triumphant in both his professional boxing match and his quest for his own father. And, like Anaya's other protagonists, he learns that the riddle of his identity is indeed in his own heart, coded deeply within him and his heritage, that he is who he is, explained to him at first by the curandera/la Llorona figure doña Tules: *tu eres tu*.

But who Abrán really is and what he represents is a mixture, a mestizo. His father, Ben, helps him learn this—and knows it first himself in his taboo interracial love as a teenager. Ben is the progenitor, as father and as writer, of this embodiment of mixed blood and mixed heritage. Ben is exemplary in fighting for the integrity of self and cultural identity—in his love for his own ever-understanding wife, Elena, in his love for Cynthia, her memory and the pledges he made to her, and in his mentorship of his son, Abrán.

Ben illustrates his values of solidarity, loyalty, and reverence for Aztlán in his poems and stories, and through the portrait of himself and Cynthia which is the pictorial proof of his paternity. Ben maps the geographical, cultural, and spiritual presence of the mythical kingdom of Aztlán in his long, epic (at times mock-epic) poem of Juan Chicapatas and Al Penco, Ben's (and Anaya's) fictive variants of Don Quixote and Sancho Panza, *norteño* folk legend, and more contemporary Cheech and Chong homeboys in search of Aztlán. Through the techniques and premises of magical realism Ben tells the story of their journey and Abrán listens and understands. Al and Juan thus work as legendary, literary alter egos. Anaya, Ben, Abrán all work out their own versions of Juan's and Al's sidekick, time-travel quest:

> Into the late hours Ben recited the story of Juan Chicapatas and Al Penco. He told how they were given the sword of life by the goddess [María Juana], the sword of life that became the tree of life. And how they were given the commandment to return to the barrios of Aztlán to help the poor and the outcast. They were to help their people by becoming troubadours, wandering minstrels, like the old cuentistas who went from village to village to tell the Chicanos their history and legends.[8]

These Chicano cultural heroes, extending from interpolated story into the protagonists of the novel itself, are accompanied by the anguish, the struggle, and the triumph of Chicanas—represented not just by the novel's various heroines, but by the spirit of La Llorona:

> "Who is la Llorona?" he [Abrán] had asked Sara when he was a child. "We, the mothers of the world, are the

crying women, because we cry when our children suffer," Sara answered. "Every woman is a Llorona."[9]

Anaya, like Ben, and through his characters, including his shadow companion, doña Loneliness, offers up that wail, that cry, both lamentation and *grito* of liberation and unity, with startling new force in his continuing saga about his Aztlán, his Albuquerque, his America.

Jimmy Santiago Baca's alter-ego hero Martín is also transcendent in his efforts to find Aztlán and its mythic harmonies in his heart, in his neighborhood, in his Albuquerque South Valley home. The Rio Grande, its waters and sand and mud and bosque nurture him, give meaning to his city, his "Burque," his Spanglishized, transvaluated sense of home where a "'56 Chevy truckita, / beat up ranckled / farm truck" translates into the good life:

> *Funny how in the Valley*
> *an old truck symbolizes prestige*
> *and in the Heights, poverty.*
>
> *Worth is determined in the Valley*
> *by age and durability,*
> *and in the Heights, by newness*
> *and impression.*
>
> *In the Valley,*
> *the atmosphere is soft and worn,*
> *things are shared and passed down.*
> *In the Heights,*
> *the air is blistered with the glaze*
> *of new cars and new homes.*[10]

The imperfect, the old and repairable, are what define Martín's life. And it is the Southside barrio, Los Ranchos de Atrisco, once (and now again) called Aztlán, that shapes his Chicano heritage, his life and landscape:

> *I study the faces of boys*
> *playing in dirt yards,*
> *and see Cuauhtémoc—images*
> *that reflect gold-cuts*
> *engraved on medallions*
> *in Spanish museums.*

Vatos,
eyes sleek with dreams,
lounge on porches
reading the flight of geese
above Río Grande,
look like Netzahualcóytl.

And thrashing out from the bosque's
wall of trees and wild bushes,
see a man in threadbare clothing,
work-worn muscles,
eyes weathered as war-drum skins,
his skin glowing with sweat
like rain on old rocks,
and here, you see
a distant relative
of Aztec warriors. (pp. 67–68)

In the *vatos*, in the muscled, poor workers, in the people of Albuquerque's South Valley is Aztlán—at once ancient and modern, peaceful and warlike.

Baca and his persona, Martín, both of them poets, speak about historical perspectives afforded by Aztlán, by Chicano history in the past and the future. For in the *vatos* of West Central and Tingley Beach is found a brotherhood of Aztlán, a kinship of Barry Lopez's literature of hope:

They lead lives trying to decide
who they are going to be—
Do they stand on Plymouth Rock
and defiantly stare down on La Raza?
Or under the fierce glare of sun
in the Aztlán desert, do they endure
their thirst for acceptance and success?
Do they celebrate Columbus day
or invent their own Día de Cortez?

These Cholos y Vatos Locos
who have refused to let themselves
be put down,
and lifted in this poem-photograph
smiling, knowing who they are,

they let the slow blue water
of their souls
seep back into the brown soil of their lives,
to speak their own lives in green,
under the harsh and punishing light of Burque.
    (pp. 84–85)

Baca's "poem photograph," his "meditation on the South Valley" of Albuquerque, and Anaya's barrio apotheosis of Clemente and Ben Chavez's quest for and discovery of Aztlán demonstrate with power and poignancy the efficacy and inspiration of landscape and myth.

In laminating and telescoping ancient Aztlán and modern Albuquerque in *Heart of Aztlán, Alburquerque*, and *Martín and Meditations of the South Valley*, Rudolfo Anaya and Jimmy Santiago Baca point the way to a truly new history, a new North American Studies, an old/new revisitation of a thicker, richer American and United States history. Together, "firme," solid in their *carnalismo*, they advance the perspectives of the New Ethnicity. It is a revisitation and revitalization much needed during this auspicious time in the wake of the quincentenary, not so much because of Columbus's "discovery" of the new world but because of his "encounter" with America, with Aztlán.

JIMMY SANTIAGO BACA: WRITING THE BORDERLANDS OF ETHNIC AND CULTURAL CRISIS

"Language made bridges of fire between me and everything I saw. Writing bridged my divided life of prisoner and free man."
—JIMMY SANTIAGO BACA, *WORKING IN THE DARK: REFLECTIONS OF A POET OF THE BARRIO*

Few contemporary authors write and live across as many ethnic, cultural, and genre, boundaries as Jimmy Santiago Baca. Consider his artistic, cultural, and ethnic identities and roles—each defined by its own set of expected and established boundaries that Baca continues to redefine, continues to cross: poet, novelist, essayist, scriptwriter, convict, honored citizen, actor, producer, lecturer, celebrity, culture hero, Chicano, Indian, southwesterner, to name just a few.

Baca faces all of his personal and professional frontiers through writing. And his writing/riding across these borders is both illustrative of times past, especially in the development of United States literature, exemplary of this time and prophetic of the courage demanded by borderland crossings in times to come.

Baca's *Working in the Dark: Reflections of a Poet of the Barrio* (1992) and his film script, *Blood In . . . Blood Out* (1993), which provides much of the focus of *Working in the Dark*, are dramatic demonstrations of the cultural and ethnic borderlands that he faces and writes across. These borderlands of personal courage and will, individuation and epiphany, frontiers of the soul and heart, mind and spirit, are played out against geographical regions mapped both matter-of-factly and transcendentally—Albuquerque's South Valley, "Burque's" Saint Anthony's orphanage, other New Mexico locales such as Santa Fe and the Llano Estacado around Estancia, and jails and state penitentiaries standing for the mythic restrictions and freedoms of the Chicano homeland known as Aztlán.

Baca's earlier, better known books of poetry, *Martín and Meditations on the South Valley* (1987) and *Black Mesa Poems* (1989), southwestern in locale, are very much embedded in the essays in *Working in the Dark* and in the film images of *Blood In . . . Blood Out*, both very much West Coast in setting and atmosphere. His work has evolved then, no longer a melded monolithic "Chicano" whole but now an organic growth of separate but blending multicultural patterns. Seen in this context, Baca the essayist and scriptwriter and filmmaker crosses from the vast frontiers of Spanish, Indio, Mejicano, Chicano New Mexico to California cool, to the fantastic imaginings of the movies and the fame and infamy associated with them, particularly in Hollywood. The incongruities of east Los Angeles, of San Quentin, of the brutalities and savagery of incarceration, set against the fawning and flattery and VIP lifestyle of a Hollywood scriptwriter, provide Baca with a whole new set of crises to write around, out of, and through. Hollywood and its seductive lure and east Los Angeles and its barrio blues, set against the hopes and dreams of a Burque boy making it big in both the East Coast worlds of poetic acclaim and the West Coast world of money and fame are not the usual, prototypical Chicano borderlands. They are, however, borderlands along a familiar path toward the American dream, a path familiar to many writers faced with the promise and the pain of American "success."

Just such choices, such crises provide the major themes of not just these recent books but also of several published interviews with Baca, which appeared in Albuquerque's *NuTimes*, *The Bloomsbury Review* of Denver, and nationally in *Esquire*. Speaking about his own personal borderlands of identity, the frontiers of writer and Chicano writer, Baca has this to say in his interview with me in *The Bloomsbury Review*, when asked if he had any advice to offer young poets, Chicano or otherwise:

> First, I'm not a spokesman for Chicanos. Second, I'm not
> a Chicano writer. I'm a writer. Tomorrow I leave for a
> tour of New York, and I'll be on various panels, some
> with Amiri Baraka, others with Galway Kinnell, some
> with Allen Ginsberg. I'll be going into prisons as well as
> to universities like Yale. I'll be going into galleries and
> community centers, Black, White, and other. Writing,
> at its best, transcends all borders. It collapses the bor-
> ders between people and becomes gift giving. It's a real
> falsehood to pigeon-hole people as "ethnic" writers.[1]

Baca's self-proclaimed identity beyond ethnic borderlands is evidenced, in part, by his publication by New Directions, publisher of such canonized writers as William Carlos Williams and Ezra Pound.

Although some Chicanos might disparage Baca as a "vendido" or sell-out, Baca's claim is not grounded so much in denial of his Chicano identity as in the affirmation of the possibility of Chicano "success." Such a pronouncement might also be viewed as a bold—albeit unpopular in certain quarters—affirmation of the universality of art. Whether viewed positively or negatively, Baca rests in this particular context smack on the frontier between acculturation and assimilation.

When asked about the borders of barrio and larger city, of power elite and criminal, of free domain and prison cell, Baca says this:

> I think that the barrio truly is the mother, the fertile mother of our folklore, our customs, and our family network. Mainstream society has chosen to ignore the barrio, doesn't give it the equal economic advantages that they do their own neighborhoods in other parts of the city. It doesn't necessarily mean that it's bad. The thing about the barrio is—a drunk is a drunk is a drunk. Up in the ritzy neighborhoods a drunk is behind doors, behind plaques, behind his job, and in a brand new Mercedes-Benz. Most of the horrendous crimes that are committed are usually committed by the psychos that live in these beautiful homes and have these wonderful lives and one day decide to go up on a tower and start shooting people. Very few Chicanos do that in a barrio. They usually go rob a store for ten dollars so they can get a fix, and they end up in prison. Then you have these other people, the judges, who have hidden agendas and have sentenced thousands and thousands of teenagers to prison, not because of their judicial insight but because of their racist views.[2]

As artist and person, Baca talks meaningfully and passionately about cultural space and about his crossings back and forth from respectability to outcast. In *Blood In . . . Blood Out*, the crossing stories of the three cousins, Meiklo as convict, Paco as policeman, and Cruz as artist-drug addict, all demonstrate the ironies of just what influences change ostensibly good lives for bad and ostensibly bad lives for good—and how acculturation is not based solely and exclusively on skin color and bloodline.

Blood In . . . Blood Out, in its varying and contradictory perspectives on La Raza identity and solidarity seems to suggest that mixed bloods can be as purely Chicano, as dedicated to cultural identities and agendas as more pure-blooded persons with assimilated roles and identities.

Rudolfo Anaya dramatizes something of the same Chicano commitment and dedication despite bloodline in *Alburquerque*. *La lucha* in a wider scope continues. It is of further irony that Baca himself in *Blood In . . . Blood Out*, cast in the role of "Gato," a killer captain to Montana, the La Honda *jefe*, is also the film's executive producer and scriptwriter.

This paradox of captive released and willfully, imaginatively returned to captivity for the purposes of film, is presented in *Working in the Dark* as a deep disorientation by Baca:

> Each day that we filmed at San Quentin, where I was surrounded by men whose sensibilities were being progressively eroded by prison society, the urge grew in me to foment a revolt: tear down the walls, herd the guards into the bay, burn down everything until nothing was left but a smoldering heap of blackened bricks and molten iron. And I was filled with a yearning to escape, to go home and live the new life I had fought so hard to make. The two worlds I inhabited then were so far apart I could find no bridge between them, no balance in myself. My disorientation was radical.[3]

Vincent Coppola's article "The Moon in Jimmy Baca," published in *Esquire* in the summer of 1993, after the wrapping of *Blood In . . . Blood Out* and after the publication of *Working in the Dark*, dramatizes just how Baca's rage and disorientation as a *vato loco* carries over into his hard-won "domesticated" life as a loving yet still longing husband and father, an esteemed poet and local celebrity, around his home near the Black Mesa south of Albuquerque and in bars in and around Burque, Bernalillo, and Santa Fe. Baca's own puzzled assessment goes this way:

> That night [in the Bernalillo jail] I ask myself, *How did I end up here?* I'm forty years old, I got a wife, two beautiful sons, a Hollywood movie, all these books. In jail with men vomiting on the floor, burping, and shitting beer? The answer? I got this . . . this thing in me like a full moon.[4]

The crises of *Working in the Dark*, of the metaphor of working in the dark, working out of the dark, out of illiteracy into literacy, out of captivity to freedom, out of anger to love, "wolf self" and "dove self," working throughout his life across the borderlands of *vato loco* and esteemed poet and darling of L.A. producers and directors—all of these borderlands are prevalent in the book's autobiographical essays. Not only does the book detail the borderlands of the Southwest and the Far West, New Mexico and California, Albuquerque and Los Angeles, it shows us the borderlands and *fronteras* and sub-cities of classes, cultures, and ethnicities within the larger seductions of L.A. itself:

> The city has a bilingual heart: in L.A. you live in two
> worlds, in celluloid shadows and hard reality. L.A. is
> South Americans whirring weed cutters on mansion
> grounds; old hippies with small boy's features toddling
> naked in their gardens at dawn; crowds of workers on
> street corners hiring out to a different employer every
> day. It is a city of the homeless sleeping in alleys on dis-
> carded couches, and single people living in fifty-room
> palaces on million-dollar-a-month budgets. There you
> become a two-world person, inhaling the intoxicating
> perfume of luxury and extravagance, and turning away
> from the piercing sight of poverty. Los Angeles miracu-
> lously replenishes itself by drinking in dreams. It's
> where life runs on opposites, greed and generosity; it's
> where the fire of envy consumes the heart of an actor
> burning to step over his fallen friend's bad luck to take
> his turn in the cold reach for stardom. (p. 114)

Using the mythic metaphors of Eve, Flora, and Satan, seductions attendant to the fall of man, Baca encapsulates his own vast hunger and ambition in a primal motive, an impulse to partake and eat of the city, to eat of life in all its crossings and borders—

> The night is aromatic with citrus dew and the ocean
> opens waves for last dreamers turned down by casting
> directors, for Mexicans yearning for home, for the
> penniless young who have come to this last coast to
> escape from their tragic secrets back home. I twine my
> python imagination around the waist of an avocado
> tree, flickering my tongue of light faintly on the skin
> of an L.A. moon. And as I bite into her tropical heart
> whose pain is a soft glow language cannot fathom nor
> the spirit, "Bite me," L.A. whispers, "Bite me." (p. 116)

Given such appetite for the unknown, such ambition, the crises of which Baca writes and which affect us all become questions, ultimately of the courage to bite, the courage to cross over, beyond bounds, the courage to face and confront the future, whether of feast or of famine, whether a land of waste or of promise. It is the hunger of art. The desire of life.

Jimmy Santiago Baca in this context writes/rides the contemporary cultural and ethnic borderlands with heroic courage—the courage of a heroic Chicano heart—not just to reclaim old lands and old myths but to till new fields, nourish new gardens, cross new frontiers of self and culture, and discover new powers of the word, of the writer as voyager, as explorer.

NOTES

Part One: Anglo Visitors
CHARLES F. LUMMIS AND ISLETA PUEBLO

1. Charles F. Lummis, *The Man Who Married the Moon and Other Pueblo Indian Folk-Stories* (New York: Century Co., 1894). Revised and enlarged as *Pueblo Indian Folk-Stories* (New York: Century Co., 1910).

2. "I was the first to apply . . . the generic christening by which it ['the million square miles which include New Mexico, Arizona, Southern California, and adjoining parts of Colorado, Utah, Texas, and Northern Mexico'] is now commonly known—THE SOUTHWEST," writes Lummis in *Mesa, Canon and Pueblo* (New York: Century Co., 1925), p. vii. *Mesa* is a revision of Lummis's fourth book, *Some Strange Corners of Our Country* (1892), and both books preview his interest in Pueblo culture as evidenced in *Pueblo Indian Folk-Stories*.

3. Lummis's career as writer, editor, photographer, amateur ethnologist, and tourist-adventurer began in 1884, at the age of twenty-five, when he decided to walk from Cincinnati, Ohio, to Los Angeles, California. Six months later, on February 1, 1885, he took a job as a city editor for the *Los Angeles Times*.

His westering experiences apparently provided the material for one of his earliest and best-known books, *A Tramp across the Continent* (1892), and gave rise to his claim that he coined the slogan "See America First."

4. If Columbus is remembered today by Native Americans and New Historians for his part in establishing processes of domination, Lummis must also be seen as contributing to Anglo-European attempts to recreate Native Americans in their own "white" image. Lummis's early versions of the "White Man's Indian" include his reports of fabricated encounters with the Pueblos and "translations" of Pueblo myths such as

those narrated by his "Don Carlos" persona. To see Lummis through present-day revisionist eyes not only as part of the history Columbus helped set in motion but as a promoter of the curio-driven kitsch of once-authentic southwestern cities like Santa Fe is not to dismiss him as an egregious interloper or as a corrupter of once pristine indigenous cultures. But his interpretations of The Southwest, *his* Southwest, were primarily intended to encourage Anglo-American tourism and boosterism.

5. In his account of the myth of "The Revenge of the Fawns," Lummis points explicitly to his own ill-founded fears and prejudices as well as to the marvel of what brought him to Isleta and his enlightenment and revaluation of Anglo attitudes: "By this time, however, having lived long among the kindly Pueblos, I had shaken off the strange, ignorant prejudice against all that is unknown—which seems to be inborn in all of us—and wondered that I could ever have believed in that brutal maxim, worthy only of worse than savages, that 'A Good Indian is a dead Indian,' for Indians are men, after all and astonishingly like the rest of us when one really comes to know them" (p. 179). Although his "confession" may sound condescending today, Lummis sought to enlighten his largely eastern, Anglo-American audience in ways that were well ahead of their time. Native Americans, it must be remembered with dismay, were not allowed to vote in the United States until 1924.

6. For a detailed account of Isleta prehistory and history in relation to other pueblos, see Florence Hawley Ellis, "Isleta Pueblo," *Handbook of North American Indians: Southwest*, Vol. 9, ed. Alfonso Ortiz (Washington, D.C.: Smithsonian Institution, 1979), pp. 351–54. Ellis dates the Laguna-Isleta phase of acculturation as taking place during the last quarter of the nineteenth century, and she views the Laguna split into progressive and conservative factions as the result of the stresses of non-Indian contact.

7. Note, for example, the Spanish names of the narrators and Lummis's own personae of "Don Carlos," "Americano," and "Por todos."

8. Marc Simmons testifies that it was during Lummis's 1888 stay in the Chaves household that he began to recover from his stroke through hunting and doing ranch chores; then he started making excursions into the mesa wilderness, excavating Indian ruins, photographing the spectacular landscape, and generally attempting to "prove that he was greater than anything that could happen to him." See Simmons, *Two Southwesterners: Charles Lummis and Amado Chaves* (San Marcos Press, 1968), p. 15. For a detailed account of Lummis's photographic methods and techniques, including the story of how Isleta water caused spotting on his prints, see Patrick T. Houlihan and Carolee Campbell, "Lummis as Photographer," *Charles F. Lummis: The Centennial Exhi-*

bition, Commemorating His Tramp across the Continent, ed. Daniela P. Moneta (Los Angeles: Southwest Museum, 1985), pp. 21–34.

9. See Lummis, *Some Strange Corners of Our Country,* p. 256.

10. See Moneta, *Charles F. Lummis,* p. 11. See also Robert E. Flemming, *Charles F. Lummis* (Boise, Idaho: Western Writers Series, No. 50, 1981), p. 11.

11. Lummis, *Some Strange Corners of Our Country,* p. 257.

12. Ibid., p. 74.

13. Elsie Clews Parsons, in "The Pueblo of Isleta: A Definitive Report," *Indian Classics Series,* Vol. 1 (Albuquerque: University of Albuquerque, 1974), p. 207, reports that Lummis's Isleta name was Paxola or star, and that he was well liked at the Pueblo.

14. Lummis's name and his reputation for benevolence are most visible and (notwithstanding his many books) most enduring in the Highland Park area of Los Angeles. There, amid the southern California ambiance of freeways, palm trees, and east L. A.'s predominantly Chicano population, are two physical legacies: Lummis's home, El Alisal, and a few blocks away, on a hill overlooking the Arroyo Seco locale of his abode, the Southwest Museum, formally opened to the public in 1914. El Alisal—named for a large native sycamore around which Lummis personally built his home out of the indigenous rocks and stones of the dry arroyo at the site—remains a testimonial to his indomitable, ever-resourceful southwestern spirit.

The Southwest Museum, one of the earliest museums in the United States dedicated to preserving and exhibiting native cultures of the Americas, demonstrates in its own compellingly visual way why Lummis was so attracted to the Native American and Hispanic cultures and their encounters with each other.

Looking at the exhibits of the southwestern rooms of the museum or perusing its collection of Lummis's manuscripts provides the visitor with a sense of his remarkable life as southwestern discoverer, observer, reporter, and mythmaker whose five years at Isleta were indispensable to him. Lummis's role as benefactor is also notable for his part in the successful restoration and preservation of the Spanish missions along California's El Camino Real.

15. See Anne M. Smith, *New Mexico Indians: Economic, Educational, and Social Problems,* Museum of New Mexico Research Records, No. 1 (Santa Fe: Museum of New Mexico, 1966), p. 101.

16. See Ellis, "Isleta Pueblo," p. 354.

17. See Joe S. Sando, *The Pueblo Indians* (San Francisco: Indian Historian Press, 1982), p. 239.

18. Ibid., p. 5.

19. Dennis Tedlock, "Introduction," *Finding the Center: Narrative Poetry of the Zuni Indians* (Lincoln: University of Nebraska Press, 1978), p. xxxi.

20. See Parsons, "Pueblo of Isleta," p. 207.

21. Hamlin Garland, "A Day at Isleta," *Hamlin Garland's Observations on the American Indian, 1895–1905*, ed. Lonnie E. Underhill and Daniel F. Littlefield, Jr. (Tucson: University of Arizona Press, 1976), p. 81.

ERNA FERGUSSON'S TRAVELS TOWARD EXOTICISM

1. Erna Fergusson, *Dancing Gods* (New York: Alfred A. Knopf, 1931); Erna Fergusson, *Our Southwest* (New York: Alfred A. Knopf, 1940); Erna Fergusson, *Erna Fergusson's Albuquerque* (Albuquerque: Merle Armitage Editions, 1947); Erna Fergusson, *Murder and Mystery in New Mexico* (Albuquerque: Merle Armitage Editions, 1948); Erna Fergusson, *New Mexico: A Pageant of Three Peoples*, 2d ed. (New York: Alfred A. Knopf, 1964). Subsequent references to *Dancing Gods* are cited parenthetically within the text. See also David A. Remley, *Erna Fergusson* (Austin: Steck-Vaughn Co., 1969). Remley finds Fergusson a difficult writer to place: "Her isolated phenomenon in the Southwest (she wrote fifty years later than the great popularizer, Charles F. Lummis, and her work is very different from that of Mary Austin and Paul Horgan). She wrote little fiction and no poetry. Hence she cannot be treated with the usual devices of literary criticism" (p. 36). Here, I attempt to view Fergusson through the tradition of "exotic" travel writing—an overlooked tradition to be sure. Ironically, it is one of the most fundamental forms used in expressing, describing, and imagining the Southwest, its Native American and Mexican-American cultures, and their interactions with Anglo Americans within the contexts of land, time, space, and climate. Remley, in the best commentary on Fergusson to date, does not pinpoint three literary techniques she used, namely: the interview, informal prose, and exaggeration, a characteristic of American humor (pp. 10–11).

2. See Rudolfo A. Anaya, "The Writer's Landscape: Epiphany in Landscape," *Latin American Literary Review* 5, no. 10 (Spring/Summer 1977): 98–102.

3. D. H. Lawrence, "New Mexico," *Phoenix: The Posthumous Papers* (New York: Viking Press, 1968), pp. 141–42.

4. Stanley Walker, "Long River, Long Book," *The New Yorker* 30 (December 4, 1954), p. 229.

5. W. Somerset Maugham, *Tellers of Tales* (New York: Doubleday, Doran, 1939), p. xxxiii ff.

6. See Harvey Fergusson, *Rio Grande* (New York: William Morrow and Co., 1955), pp. 286–87.

7. Edmund Wilson, "Zuni," *Red, Black, Blond, and Olive* (New York: Oxford University Press, 1956), pp. 3–68.

HARVEY FERGUSSON'S LEGACY

1. Stanley Walker, "Long River, Long Book," *The New Yorker* 30 (December 4, 1954), p. 234.

2. See Robert F. Gish, "Calliope and Clio: Paul Horgan's River Muses," *Southwest Review* 69 (Winter 1984): 2–15.

3. Frank D. Reeve, "A Letter to Clio," *New Mexico Historical Review* 31 (April 1956): 132.

4. James West Davidson and Mark Hamilton Lytle, eds., *After the Fact: The Art of Historical Detection* (New York: Alfred A. Knopf, 1982), p. vi.

5. Ibid., p. vi.

6. Ibid., p. vii.

7. Ibid.

8. Quoted from the galleys of the fourth edition of *Great River*, which appeared in spring 1985.

9. *The American Mercury* 23 (May 1931): xxvii.

10. Ibid.

11. Harvey Fergusson, *Rio Grande* (New York: William Morrow and Company, 1955), p. 293. All subsequent references in the text are to this edition and are cited parenthetically.

12. Letter to Robert F. Gish, April 9, 1984.

13. See William T. Pilkington, *Harvey Fergusson* (Boston: Twayne Publishers, 1975), p. 109. For another account, particularly of the "democratic" and "humanistic" Pueblo Indians, see Tony Hillerman's *Rio Grande* (Portland: Graphic Arts Center Publishing Co., 1975), pp. 20–21.

14. James K. Folsom, *Harvey Fergusson* (Austin: Steck-Vaughn, 1969), p. 29.

15. Maxwell Anderson, "Rio Grande," *The Nation* 137 (April 16, 1933): 190–91.

16. Arthur G. Pettit, "The Decline and Fall of the New Mexican Great House in the Novels of History of Harvey Fergusson: A Classical Example of Anglo-American Ethnocentricity," *New Mexico Historical Review* 51 (July 1976): 188–89.

17. Cecil Robinson, *With the Ears of Strangers: The Mexican in American Literature* (Tucson: University of Arizona Press, 1963), p. 82.

18. Paul Horgan, "New Mexico," *The Yale Review* 23 (September 1933): 211-13.

19. See R. L. Duffus, "Where America's Past Lives On," *New York Times Book Review*, July 23, 1933; Edwin L. Sabin, "The Old Southwest," *The Saturday Review of Literature*, August 12, 1933.

20. The photographs of Alex Harris and the writing of Robert Coles in *The Old Ones of New Mexico* (Albuquerque: University of New Mexico Press, 1973) attempt to capture the spirit of these same people.

21. Sabine R. Ulibarri, *Mi abuela fumaba puros: y otro cuentos de Tierra Amarilla* (Berkeley: Quinto Sol, 1977), p. 159.

22. Marta Weigle, *Brothers of Light/Brothers of Blood: The Penitentes of the Southwest* (Albuquerque: University of New Mexico Press, 1976), p. 268.

WITTER BYNNER, POET IN ADOBIA

1. James Kraft, "Introduction," *Selected Letters*, ed. Kraft (New York: Farrar, Straus and Giroux, 1981), p. ix.

2. Literary historians of the American West generally give little acknowledgment to Bynner as a western or southwestern poet. Tom Trusky lists him merely as a New Mexico poet "of note during the twenties and thirties" and observes that "Bynner's *Indian Earth* (1929) is . . . of regional import . . ." See Trusky, "Western Poetry, 1850-1950)," *A Literary History of the American West*, ed. Thomas J. Lyon et al. (Fort Worth: Texas Christian University Press, 1987), 187.

3. "Witter Bynner Dies:Literary Giant," *Santa Fe New Mexican* (hereafter cited as *SFNM*), June 2, 1968. See also the newspaper's earlier tribute: John MacGregor, "Witter Bynner Observes 85th Birthday Quietly," *SFNM*, August 10, 1966.

4. Santa Fe writer Dorothy Hughes offers this account of Bynner and the Santa Fe group in the thirties and early forties: "In those days it seemed as if everyone played piano. There was no TV, of course, and radio didn't supplant music and singing. Hal [Harold Witter Bynner] played the piano—loudly if not too artistically—and sang wonderful bawdy English music hall songs in good Cockney. . . . Hal was the host to all who came to town from the East, it was at his museum-piece house that one met all the writers and artists and VIPs who visited Santa Fe. . . . There was, of course a nucleus of Santa Feans who were part of the group, members of old families, like Oteros and Bergeres, and all the other old Santa Feans. There were also the poor young artists and writers who had come here [Santa Fe] to live to a sizable extent to wait out the depression. The depression did not extend to Santa

Fe, which was even more out of the world in the '30s than it is today, and it's still pretty far removed from the hurly burly. Santa Fe was always a high-priced town, because its uniqueness brought outlanders to visit, and prices did not decrease in the depression—that is what I mean when I say the depression didn't hit here. I can't remember all names to be sure, but the inner circle and permanent members of the crowd included Haniel Long and his wife Alice, Lynn Riggs—who lived in the chicken coop, so-called, at Margaretta Dietrich's apartment community; Frank Applegate and family, he built the Camino practically single-handed, was a fine-folklorists writer, Dolly and John Sloan; in early days so many artists always—Willard Nash, Andrew Dasburg, Randall Davy . . . , Frieda Lawrence down from Taos . . . , Mabel (Dodge Luhan) from Taos on occasion. Mabel's son was married to Alice (now Rossin), daughter of Alice Corbin and William Penhallow Henderson. Big Alice was one of the founders of *Poetry* magazine and Willie a fine painter and architect, Little Alice is important in the Fine Arts Museum here. All I have mentioned lived here or in Taos in those days. The Sloans spent the winter in New York, and dear Lynn practically commuted the continent—Hollywood and New York, once he hit it on Broadway. . . . Paul [Horgan] was of course a member of this permanent crowd although he didn't live here. There are many, many more but it would take a week of contemplation to recall all of them. My husband and I were young marrieds then. Paul and Lynn and of course little Alice were the younger set—but there were never any age barriers or ethnic barriers in Old Santa Fe." Letter to Robert F. Gish from Dorothy B. Hughes, Santa Fe, July 24, 1979.

5. Paul Horgan, *Approaches to Writing* (Middletown, Conn.: Wesleyan University Press, 1988), p. 251.

6. Horgan, "Critical Essay," *Selected Poems by Witter Bynner*, ed. Robert Hunt (New York: Alfred A. Knopf, 1943), p. 274.

7. See Bynner to Alice Corbin Henderson, Jan. 21, 1922, in Kraft, *Selected Letters*, pp. 85–86; Bynner says, "I have been giving a comprehensive talk on 'A Year in China' or 'The Year of China,' whichever you prefer as a title. It contains both amusement and meat. I illuminate it here and there with Chinese poems" (p. 85). Also, see Martha Weigle and Kyle Fiore, eds., *Santa Fe and Taos: The Writer's Era*, pp. 10, 18; and *New Mexico Artists and Writers: A Celebration, 1940*, A Special Republication of the June 26, 1940, Artists and Writers Edition of *The Santa Fe New Mexican* (Santa Fe: Ancient City Press, 1982), p. 15.

8. Alice Bullock, "A Portrait of a Genius," *Pasatiempo*, Santa Fe, N.M. (April 7, 1968), p. 1. Subsequent references in the text are cited parenthetically.

9. Robert Hunt, "Editor's Foreword," *Selected Poems*, p. xvii. Subsequent references are cited parenthetically.

10. Bynner, "A City of Change," *Prose Pieces* (hereafter cited parenthetically in the text as *PP*), ed. James Kraft (New York: Farrar, Straus, Giroux, 1979), pp. 45-46. Bynner's poetic rendering of Santa Fe, similarly highlighting the theme of change in the "royal," and "ancient" city, is found in "Santa Fe": "Here is a mountain-town that prays and dances / With something left, thought much besides must fail, / Of the ancient faith and wisdom of St. Francis." This poem first appeared in *Against the Cold* (1940); later it served as the first song in Ned Rorem, *The Santa Fe Songs: Twelve Poems of Witter Bynner for Medium Voice, Violin, Viola, Cello and Piano* (Boosey and Hawkes, 1980), commissioned by the Santa Fe Chamber Music Festival for its 1980 season and first performed at the Greer Garson Theatre, College of Santa Fe, July 27, 1980. The songs were composed by Rorem in Nantucket and New York, December 1979-March 1980.

11. Horgan, *Roswell Museum Bulletin* (Roswell, N.M.), Vol. 3, No. 1 (Fall 1954), p. 2.

12. M. H. Abrams, *A Glossary of Literary Terms* (New York: Holt, Rinehart and Winston, 1988), pp. 112-13.

13. Lorraine Carr, "It Happened in Santa Fe," *Albuquerque Tribune*, (June 5, 1968), describes Bynner's funeral this way: "Jane Bauman gave a beautiful eulogy. She spoke of this informal gathering as being exactly as if Witter himself had planned it. Then the group sat silent and spellbound when a tape recording was played. It was Witter Bynner's clear strong voice reading his poem 'A Dance for Rain (Cochiti)' and his favorite poem, 'Epithalamium and Elegy.' It was a short simple memorial. We did not feel that we had attended a funeral, rather we had spent a few minutes with Witter Bynner. . . . Members of the art colony, writers and friends came to say goodbye to Witter—Will Shuster, Teresa and Josef Bakos, Eugenia Shonnard and Elenor Scott. . . . From Albuquerque came Dr. Tom (T. M.) Pearce and his wife. The nurses who attended the poet during his long illness, the care takers in the house and garden were placed in a special pew in the chapel."

14. See Hunt, *Selected Poems by Witter Bynner*, p. 118.

15. Bynner, *Indian Earth* (New York: Alfred A. Knopf, 1930), p. 65.

PART TWO: INDIAN VOICES
THE WORD MEDICINE OF JAMES WELCH

1. James Welch, *Winter in the Blood* (New York: Bantam Books, 1974). All subsequent references to the novel are from this edition and

cited parenthetically. Other critics who have pointed to the comic aspects of the novel include: Charles R. Larson, *American Indian Fiction* (Albuquerque: University of New Mexico Press, 1978); Alan R. Velie, *Four American Indian Literary Masters* (Norman: University of Oklahoma Press, 1982); Peter Wild, *James Welch* (Boise: Western Writers Series, 1983); and William F. Smith, "*Winter in the Blood*: The Indian Cowboy as Everyman," *Michigan Academician*, 10 (Winter 1978).

2. In trying to understand how tragedy and comedy mingle in *Winter in the Blood*, Northrop Frye's scheme of four "Pregeneric plots," his four "Mythos or generic plots," provide one context. In Frye's system, *Winter in the Blood* might be regarded most generally as representative of "the mythos of winter: irony and satire." Frye says, "Tragedy and comedy contrast rather than blend, and so do romance and irony, the champions respectively of the ideal and the actual. On the other hand, comedy blends insensibly into satire at one extreme and into romance at the other; romance may be comic or tragic; tragic extends from high romance to bitter and ironic realism." See Northrop Frye, *Anatomy of Criticism* (Princeton, N.J.: Princeton University Press, 1957), p. 162. Defining his "mythos of winter," Frye says, "the central principle of ironic myth is best approached as a parody of romance: the application of romantic mythical forms to a more realistic content which fits them in unexpected ways" (p. 223). And so it is with *Winter in the Blood*.

3. James Welch, *The Death of Jim Loney* (New York: Harper and Row, 1979), p. 179. Subsequent references to this edition are cited parenthetically in the text.

4. James Willard Schultz (1859–1947) was a writer and trader who first traveled to Montana in 1877. He settled among the Blackfeet near the Canadian border and married a woman named Natahki. After her death he moved to Los Angeles and became literary critic for the *Los Angeles Times*. He wrote many books and his articles often were published in George Bird Grinnell's *Forest and Stream*. His book of stories, *Blackfeet Tales of Glacier National Park*, appeared in 1916.

5. "An Interview with James Welch," in *James Welch*, ed. Ron McFarland (Lewiston, Idaho: Confluence Press, 1986), p. 5.

6. James Welch, *Fools Crow* (New York: Viking Penguin, 1986), p. 245. Subsequent references are cited parenthetically.

7. See Larry McMurtry, "Ever a Bridegroom: Reflections on the Failure of Texas Literature," *The Texas Observer* (Oct. 23, 1981), 1, 8–18. See also Gerald D. Nash and Richard W. Etulain, eds., *The Twentieth Century West: Historical Interpretations* (Albuquerque: University of New Mexico Press, 1989).

8. After his revisitation of nineteenth-century Native American

Blackfeet experience in *Fools Crow*, Welch set out to do something different, something not especially from his own Indian background. His description of his wishes now has that special ironic ring of hindsight, for in *The Indian Lawyer* Welch failed completely to escape his background, either as a Native American or as a Native American parole-board member, and yet he succeeded in adapting it to the new concerns of the new West, the new history. When asked by an interviewer, in 1984, if he ever saw himself "writing a novel that would not be from your Indian experience and your personal background," Welch replied: "I am on the Parole Board here in Montana, and we go to the prison every month for these meetings, interviews for prisoners. I've often thought, prisoners have the most fantastically interesting backgrounds that you can possibly imagine. We go through probably eight cases a month, and each one of them is incredible. So I often think, 'God I'd like to write a novel about this experience,' but I don't know which point of view I would tackle—the member of the parole board?—or would it be the prison situation?—or would it be an inmate's standpoint? So, although I wouldn't know how to go about that, I could conceive of writing a novel based upon that experience, which wouldn't be my own or my background." McFarland, "Interview with James Welch," pp. 16–17.

9. James Welch, *The Indian Lawyer* (New York: W. W. Norton and Company, 1990), p. 160. Subsequent references are cited parenthetically.

LISTENING TO RAY A. YOUNG BEAR

1. Ray A. Young Bear, "the birds are housed in a small glass house," unpublished poem.

2. The few poems considered in this essay are chosen from both published and—at the time this piece was first published—unpublished verse. The unpublished poems were part of Young Bear's Individual Studies Thesis in creative expression, completed in 1976 at the University of Northern Iowa, and some, but not all, were included in his first book of poems, published by Harper and Row, entitled *Winter of the Salamander*.

3. Richard Hugo, "Introduction," "Young American Indian Poets," *American Poetry Review* 2, No. 6 (November-December 1973), p. 22.

4. A selected bibliography of his published works is as follows: Ray A. Young Bear, "Another Face," "War Walking Near," "These Horses Came," "Songs of Life," *Come to Power*, ed. Dick Lourie (New York: Crossing Press, 1974), pp. 17–21; "A Woman's Name," *Partisan Review* 43, No. 2 (1976), p. 260; "Before Leaving Me, the Poem: Eagle Butte and Black River Falls," *The Great Circumpolar Bear Cult*, No. 1 (1976), pp. 13–15; "The Crow-Children Walk My Circles in the Snow," *Seneca*

Review 2, No. 2 (December 1971), pp. 5–6; "Four Poems," *Decotah Territory*, No. 12 (Winter-Spring 1975–1976), p. 5; "Four Songs of Life," "Morning-Talking Mother," "Through Lifetime," *The Portable North American Indian Reader*, ed. Frederick W. Turner III (New York: Viking Press, 1974), pp. 610–13; "Four Songs of Life," "Morning-Talking Mother," "Through Lifetime," *South Dakota Review* 9 (Summer 1971), pp. 38–40; "In Disgust and in Response," *Poetry Northwest* 17, No. 2 (Summer 1976), pp. 18–20; "In Dream: The Privacy of Sequence," "Waiting to be Fed," *American Poetry Review* 2, No. 6 (November–December 1973), pp. 25–26; "The Last Dream," "From His Dream," *Sun Tracks* 2, No. 2 (Spring 1976), pp. 12–13; "Painted Visions," "War Walking Near," *The Phoenix* 3, No. 2 (Winter 1970), pp. 92–93; "One Chip of Human Bone," *The Way*, ed. Shirley Hill Witt and Stan Steiner (New York: Alfred A. Knopf, 1972), p. 139; "The Place of O," "What We Can," "The Place of V," "Before the Actual Cold," "The Way the Bird Sat," "In Dream: The Privacy of Sequence," "Waiting to be Fed," "Another Face," "Celebration," "The Miss," "Coming Back Home," "Train Made of Stone," "Rushing," "The Crow-Children Walk My Circles in the Snow," "The Cook," "A Remembrance of a Color Inside a Forest," "This House," "Black Dog," "War Walking Near," "A Poem for Diane Wakoski," *Carriers of the Dream Wheel*, ed. Duane Niatum (New York: Harper and Row, 1975), pp. 255–87; "The Way the Bird Sat," *Northwest Review* 13, No. 2 (1973), pp. 30–34; "Through Lifetime," *From the Belly of the Shark*, ed. Walter Lowenfels (New York: Vintage Books, 1973), p. 72; "Windows," *Poetry Now* 2, No. 1, p. 28; "Wrong Kind of Love," "Warrior Dreams," "One Chip of Human Bone," "Empty Streams of Autumn," "The Listening Rock," *Voices from Wah'Kon-Tah*, ed. Robert K. Dodge and Joseph S. McCullough (New York: International Publishers, 1974), pp. 131–36; see also Angeline Jacobsen, *Contemporary Native American Literature* (Metuchen, N.J.: Scarecrow Press, 1977), pp. 125–31.

5. Duane Niatum, ed., *Carriers of the Dream Wheel* (New York: Harper and Row, 1975), p. 256.

6. Fred McTaggart, *Wolf that I Am: In Search of the Red Earth People* (Boston: Houghton Mifflin Co., 1976), p. 96.

7. Ibid., p. 95.

8. Ray A. Young Bear, "In Disgust and in Response," *Poetry Northwest* 17, No. 2 (Summer 1976), p. 20. Subsequent quotations of this version of the poem are cited parenthetically.

9. Ray A. Young Bear, "Before Leaving Me, the Poem: Eagle Butte and Black River Falls," *The Great Circumpolar Bear Cult*, No. 1 (Summer 1976), p. 15.

10. Ray A. Young Bear, "Four Songs of Life," *The Portable North American Indian Reader,* ed. Frederick W. Turner III (New York: Viking Press, 1974), p. 610.

11. Ibid., p. 611.

12. Ibid.

13. Ibid., p. 612.

14. Ray A. Young Bear, "The Last Dream," *Sun Tracks* 2, No. 2 (Spring 1976), p. 12.

15. Ray A. Young Bear, "A Pool of Water, a Reflection of a Summer" (Individual Studies Thesis, University of Northern Iowa, 1976). This version of the poem remains unpublished.

16. Vine Deloria, Jr., "Foreword," *Voices from Wah'Kon-Tah* (New York: International Publishers, 1974), p. 11.

17. The poems discussed in this section were part of Young Bear's Individual Studies thesis in creative expression completed in 1976 at the University of Northern Iowa. Much of this work appeared as part of *Winter of the Salamander,* published by Harper and Row. Also, see Robert F. Gish, "Memory and Dream in the Poetry of Ray A. Young Bear," *Minority Voices* 2, No. 1 (Spring 1978), pp. 21–30.

18. See *Western American Literature* 11, No. 4 (Winter 1977), p. 361.

19. Merle Brown, "Poetic Listening," *New Literary History* 10, No. 1 (Autumn 1978), p. 125.

20. Ray A. Young Bear, *The Invisible Musician* (Duluth, Minn.: Holy Cow! Press, 1990), p. 20.

21. Ibid., p. 41.

22. Ray A. Young Bear, *Black Eagle Child: The Facepaint Narratives* (Iowa City: University of Iowa Press, 1992), p. 144.

PART THREE: CHICANO VISTAS
LA LLORONA, MAGIC REALISM, AND THE FRONTIER

1. See George R. McMurray, "Magical Realism in Spanish Fiction," *Colorado State Review* 8, No. 2 (Spring-Summer 1981), p. 7.

2. Ibid., p. 8.

3. See Edwin Fussell, *Frontier: American Literature and the American West* (Princeton, N.J.: Princeton University Press, 1965), p. 7.

4. Janis P. Stout, *The Journey Narrative in American Literature* (Westport, Conn.: Greenwood Press, 1983), p. 6.

5. Fussell, *Frontier,* p. 17.

6. McMurray, "Magical Realism," p. 18.

7. See Wayne Ude, "North American Magical Realism," *Colorado State Review* 8, No. 2 (Spring–Summer 1981), pp. 21–30.

8. See Kristin Herzog, *Women, Ethnics, and Exotics* (Knoxville: University of Tennessee Press, 1983). Herzog offers a compelling case for rediscovering the significance of so-called dark and primitive fictional female characters and their ostensibly inferior characterization relative to men. Herzog finds female characters as they are actually portrayed to be equal if not superior to male characters.

9. See Marilynn Preston, "Evil Women on TV a Reflection of Reality," *Iowa TV, Des Moines Register*, Sunday, February 12, 1984, p. 6.

10. Ray John de Aragón, *The Legend of La Llorona* (Las Vegas, N.M.: Pan American Publishing Co., 1980). Subsequent references are cited parenthetically in the text.

11. Sabine R. Ulibarrí, *Tierra Amarilla* (Albuquerque: University of New Mexico Press, 1971); and *Mi Abuela Fumaba Puros* (Berkeley: Quinto Sol Publications, 1977).

12. Ulibarrí, *Mi Abuela Fumaba Puros*, p. 51.

13. See T. M. Pearce, *New Mexico Place Names* (Albuquerque: University of New Mexico Press, 1965), p. 106.

14. Orlando Romero, *Nambé—Year One* (Berkeley: Tonatiuh International, 1976), pp. 61–62. Subsequent references are cited parenthetically in the text.

15. Rudolfo A. Anaya, *Bless Me, Ultima* (Berkeley: Quinto Sol, 1972); *Heart of Aztlán* (Berkeley: Editorial Justa, 1976); *Tortuga* (Berkeley: Editorial Justa, 1979); *The Silence of the Llano* (Berkeley: Tonatiuh—Quinto Sol International, 1982); *The Legend of La Llorona* (Berkeley: Tonatiuh—Quinto Sol International, 1984); *Alburquerque* (Albuquerque: University of New Mexico Press, 1992).

16. See Robert F. Gish, "Curanderismo and Witchery in the Fiction of Rudolfo A. Anaya: The Novel as Magic," *New Mexico Humanities Review* 2, No. 2 (Summer 1979), 5–13.

17. Anaya, *Heart of Aztlán*, pp. 128–29.

18. Anaya, *Tortuga*, p. 55. Subsequent references are cited parenthetically in the text.

19. Anaya, *Silence of the Llano*, p. 28.

20. Ibid., p. 29.

21. Ibid.

CURANDERISMO AND WITCHERY IN THE FICTION OF RUDOLFO A. ANAYA

1. See the back cover of Rudolfo A. Anaya, *Bless Me, Ultima* (Berkeley: Quinto Sol, 1972). Subsequent references are cited parenthetically in the text.

2. C. G. Jung, *The Basic Writings of C. G. Jung* (New York: Modern Library, 1959), p. 160.

3. Ibid., p. 158.

4. Ibid., p. 179.

5. Rudolfo A. Anaya, *Heart of Aztlán* (Berkeley: Editorial Justa, 1976), p. 49.

6. Ibid., p. 50.

7. Ibid., p. 127.

8. Ibid., pp. 128–29.

9. Ari Kiev, *Curanderismo: Mexican-American Folk Psychiatry* (New York: The Free Press, 1972), p. 163.

AMERICA AS AZTLÁN: LANDSCAPE, MYTH, AND ETHNICITY IN RUDOLFO ANAYA'S *HEART OF AZTLÁN* AND *ALBUQUERQUE*, AND JIMMY SANTIAGO BACA'S *MARTÍN AND MEDITATIONS ON THE SOUTH VALLEY*

1. Among Anglo-American literary artists who have focused on the crucial relationships between landscape, myth, and ethnic presence, D. H. Lawrence and William Carlos Williams are two of the most vehement, the most lyrical "historian/critics," with Lawrence concentrating upon the "classic" United States authors and Williams dealing with essentially noncanonical but nevertheless important writers and historical figures.

Williams's poetic narrative histories, his reimagined retellings of the lives and events involved in the making of North American history, provide a seminal text, an early twentieth-century map to follow in establishing a "new ethnicity, a "new history" of aborigines and pioneers, of Native Americans and Anglo Europeans, and other multicultural interactions.

Although Williams declared his plottings of event and character during the period of North American discovery and settlement as being "in the American grain," they were, in the context of his day, very much "against the American grain"—which, for Williams, largely meant they were against the Puritan grain and in the grain of the indigenous, the autochthonous.

It is his impassioned iconoclasm, his assumption of a "minority" attitude, his demystifying and demythologizing of the traditional Eurocentric gods and heroes, his remythologizing and reevaluating of accepted idols and icons which still bring new meaning to the fictions (to the 1920s version of "new" history) of the American frontier and the American West.

Williams, as poet and as historian, was deeply influenced by Native American oral traditions—to which he alludes in *Paterson* as the aboriginal, "Satyric dance"—and his work also embodies incarnations and

incantations of myth in ways not yet fully realized and explained by
most critics. For a study that attempts to deal with this topic more fully,
see Robert F. Gish, *William Carlos Williams: The Short Fiction* (Boston:
G. K. Hall, 1989).

D. H. Lawrence focused a similar kind of passionate attention (also,
as with Williams, in the 1920s) on the American Southwest. *Studies in
Classic American Literature* was published in 1923 and *In the American
Grain* appeared in 1925, so Lawrence and Williams knew each other's
work. Lawrence even gave Williams's *American Grain* a favorable review.

Mary Austin, now deservedly receiving new biographical scrutiny,
was obsessed, like Williams and Lawrence, with the old myths, the old
rhythms of Native American and Hispanic language and story, linked
spiritually to the Southwest as a land of religious "nodality," a place at
once mythic and prophetic. Shelley Armitage, in her splendid commentary on Austin by way of a preface to Peggy Pond Church's biography
of Austin, makes the point that Austin's *The American Rhythm* (1923)
"antedates William Carlos Williams's *In the American Grain* and anticipates Williams's and other American writers' reclaiming of vital local,
regional, and indigenous elements." Armitage, "Mary Austin: Writing
Nature," in Peggy Pond Church, *Wind's Trail: The Early Life of Mary
Austin* (Santa Fe: Museum of New Mexico Press, 1990), p. 24.

Austin's need for an empathic union with nature, myth, and landscape and its rhythms as a means toward physical and emotional health,
and as a subject for the artist, for aesthetic inspiration and the harmony
of truth and beauty, provides the basis of method and message for Anaya
and Baca. They should not, however, be viewed as coming in the wake of
the tradition of Lawrence, Williams, and Austin—certainly not exclusively so. Anaya and Baca's perspectives on Aztlán and the Southwest and
on Albuquerque as Aztlán are not only the result of a shared heritage, but
are part of an even older tradition of "writing the land" or "writing nature."

Frederick Turner, in his *Spirit of Place: The Making of an American
Literary Landscape* (San Francisco: Sierra Club Books, 1989), attributes
much of the nineteenth-century realignment of landscape and myth, of
modern "regionalism," to Hamlin Garland, who in following Joseph
Kirkland's advice to write about his heritage, about the prairie, discovered himself and his subject in such works as *Main-Travelled Roads*
(1891) and in his subsequent practice of the aesthetic theory he dubbed
"veritism." In Turner's words, "Garland rang an American change on
this [Hippolyte Taine's declaration that the "truly original artist"
worked "with the materials of his local environment"] by making an
artistic virtue of what had often been a term of opprobrium. The trouble with American art, he wrote, was not that it was too provincial but

that it wasn't provincial enough. It did not have its roots firmly in the soils of specific places" (p. 9). See also Robert F. Gish, *Hamlin Garland: The Far West* (Boise, Idaho: Western Writers Series, 1976).

Before Garland, of course, there was Emerson, and before him the whole tradition of the mythological and numinous—of the Old World before Christianity, where, Turner reminds us, people "had lived in a numinous landscape spangled with sacred markers and sacred places. The land itself was believed to be alive and under the protection of numina, guardian spirits" (p. 12). It was the Judeo-Christian, monotheistic tradition, Turner adds, that cast out the numina, the spirits of place.

2. Ray Gonzalez, "Landscapes of the Interior: The Literature of Hope—An Interview with Barry Lopez," *The Bloomsbury Review* (January/February 1990), p. 8.

3. Demetria Martínez, "Poet Started Expressing His Culture in Prison," *Albuquerque Journal*, November 19, 1990, p. G-8.

4. Ibid.

5. Rudolfo A. Anaya, "Sale of Atrisco Land Grant Means Loss of History, Tradition," *Albuquerque Journal*, January 3, 1983, p. B-3.

6. Rudolfo A. Anaya, "The Writer's Landscape: Epiphany in Landscape," *Latin American Literary Review* 5, No. 10 (Spring/Summer 1977), pp. 99–100.

7. Rudolfo A. Anaya, *Bless Me, Ultima* (Berkeley: Quinto Sol, 1972), pp. 10–11.

8. Rudolfo A. Anaya, *Alburquerque* (Albuquerque: University of New Mexico Press, 1992), pp. 206–7. See also Robert F. Gish, *"Zia Summer," The Bloomsbury Review*, vol. 15/6 (Nov./Dec.), pp. 22–23.

9. Ibid., p. 24.

10. Jimmy Santiago Baca, *Martín and Meditations on the South Valley* (New York: New Directions, 1987), p. 59. Subsequent references are cited parenthetically in the text.

JIMMY SANTIAGO BACA: WRITING THE BORDERLANDS OF ETHNIC AND CULTURAL CRISIS

1. Robert F. Gish, "Bridges of Fire: An Interview with Jimmy Santiago Baca," *The Bloomsbury Review* 12, No. 5 (July/August 1992), p. 20.

2. Ibid., p. 7.

3. Jimmy Santiago Baca, *Working in the Dark: Reflections of a Poet of the Barrio* (Santa Fe: Red Crane Books, 1992), p. 17. Subsequent references are cited parenthetically in the text.

4. Vincent Coppola, "The Moon in Jimmy Baca," *Esquire* (June 1993), p. 48.

INDEX